Disney LATEST HITS

Beauty and the Beast
20 Beauty and the Beast
2 Days in the Sun
8 Evermore
14 How Does a Moment Last Forever

Coco
28 Remember Me (Ernesto de la Cruz)
32 Un Poco Loco
25 The World Es Mi Familia

Frozen
38 Do You Want to Build a Snowman?
47 Let It Go

Lava
56 Lava

Moana
65 How Far I'll Go
70 We Know the Way
74 You're Welcome

Tangled
82 I See the Light
88 I've Got a Dream

ISBN 978-1-5400-4154-8

HAL•LEONARD®

Visit Hal Leonard Online at
www.halleonard.com

Contact us:
Hal Leonard
7777 West Bluemound Road
Milwaukee, WI 53213
Email: info@halleonard.com

In Europe, contact:
Hal Leonard Europe Limited
42 Wigmore Street
Marylebone, London, W1U 2RN
Email: info@halleonardeurope.com

In Australia, contact:
Hal Leonard Australia Pty. Ltd.
4 Lentara Court
Cheltenham, Victoria, 3192 Australia
Email: info@halleonard.com.au

DAYS IN THE SUN
from BEAUTY AND THE BEAST

Music by ALAN MENKEN
Lyrics by TIM RICE

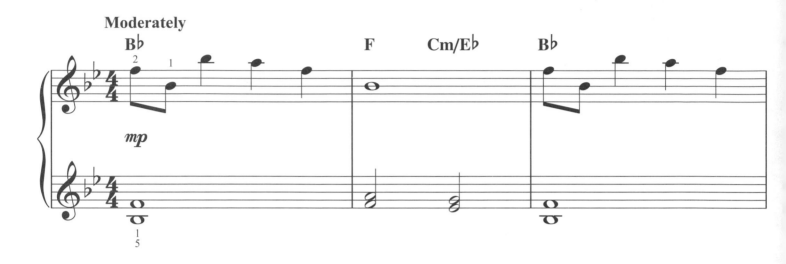

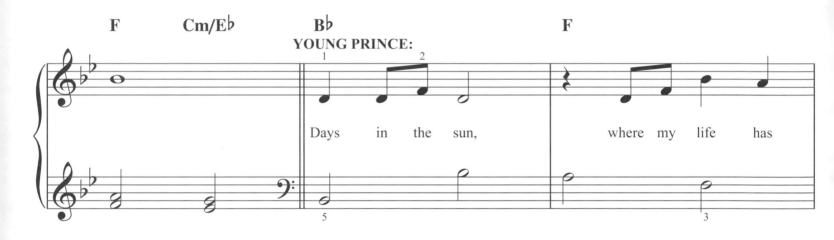

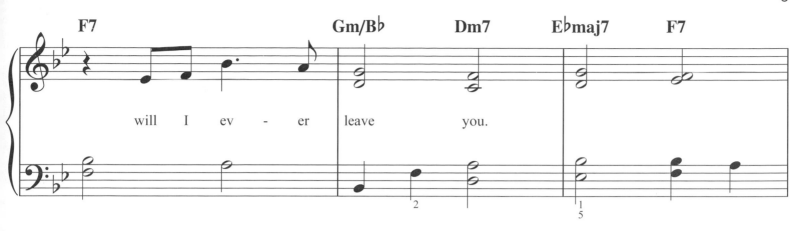

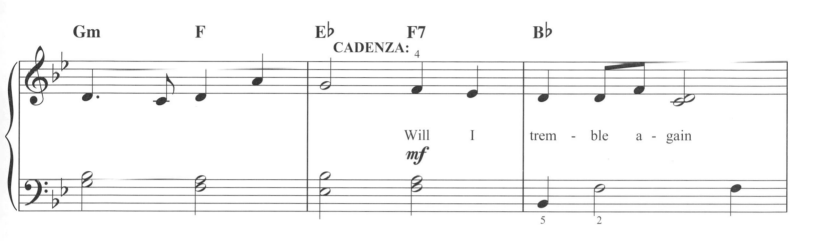

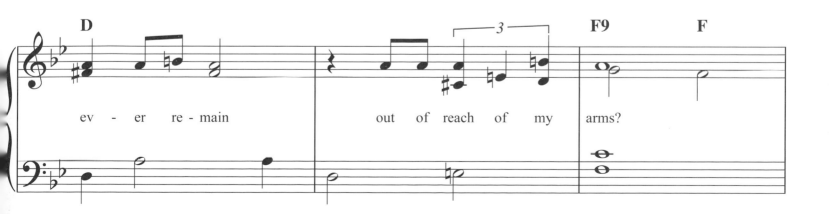

MRS. POTTS:

All those days in the sun: what I'd give to re-

live just one, un - do what's done

and bring back the light. MADAME GARDEROBE: Oh,

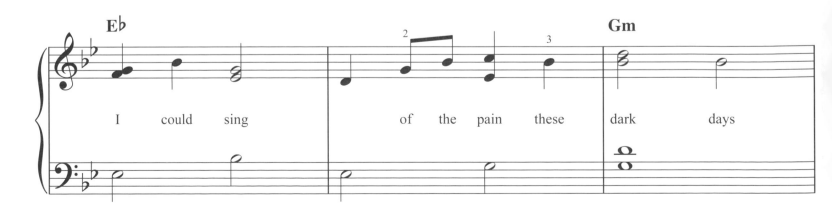

I could sing of the pain these dark days

bring, the spell we're un - der.

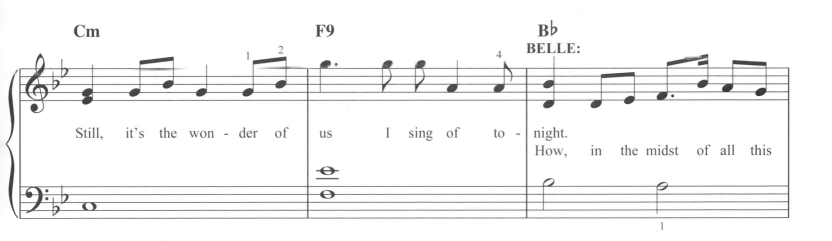

Still, it's the won - der of us I sing of to - night.
How, in the midst of all this

sor - row, can so much hope and love en - dure? I was

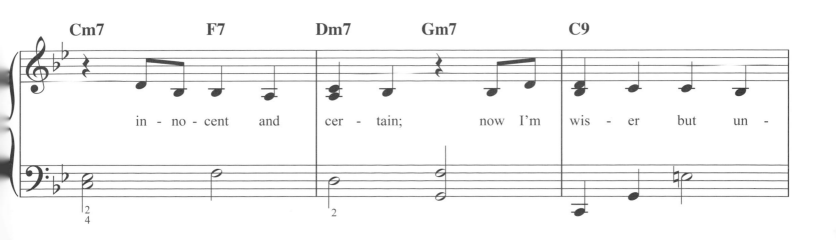

in - no - cent and cer - tain; now I'm wis - er but un -

6

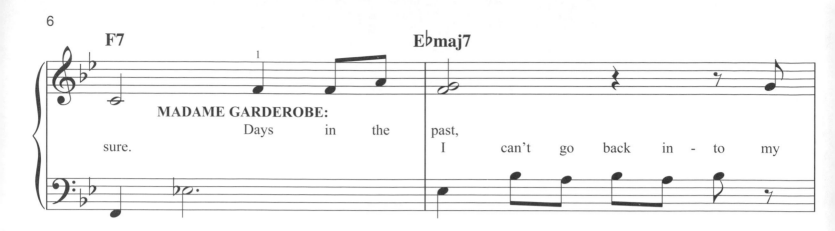

MADAME GARDEROBE:

Days in the past,
sure.

I can't go back in-to my

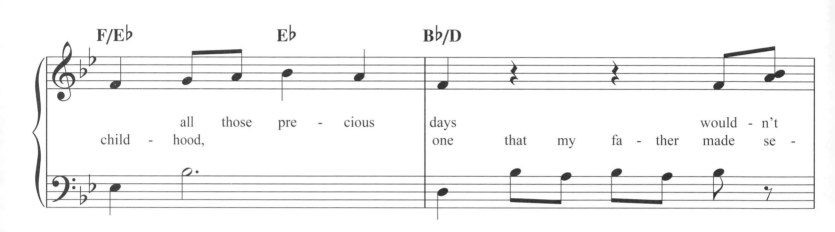

all those pre - cious days
child - hood, one that my fa - ther made se -

would - n't

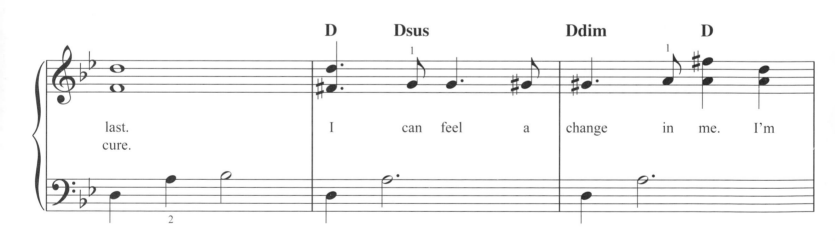

last.
cure.

I can feel a change in me. I'm

strong - er now, but still not free.
rall.

ALL:
Days in the sun
f *a tempo*

5

will re - turn, we must be - lieve, as

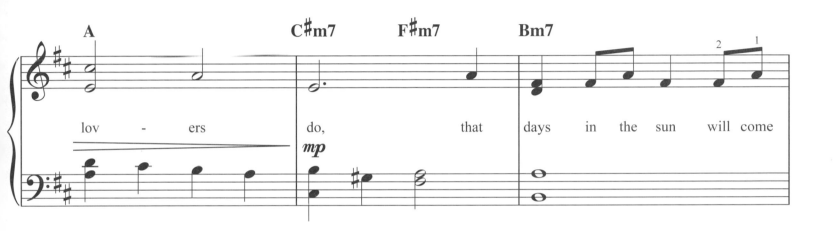

lov - ers do, that days in the sun will come

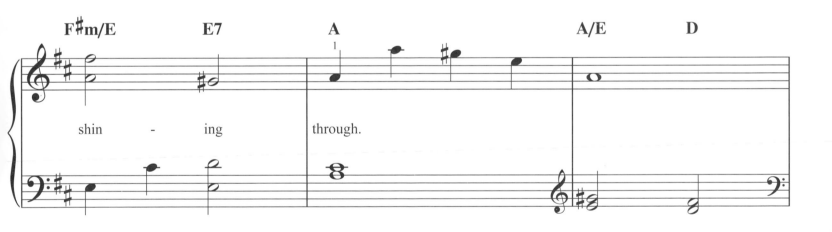

shin - ing through.

molto rit.

EVERMORE
from BEAUTY AND THE BEAST

Music by ALAN MENKEN
Lyrics by TIM RICE

Moderately slow, with freedom

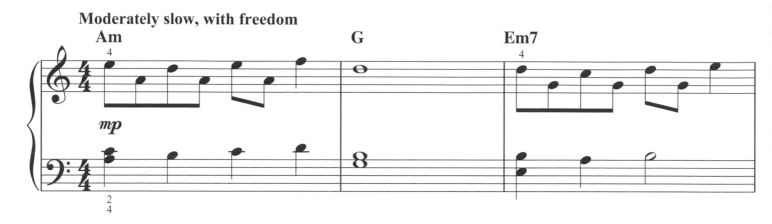

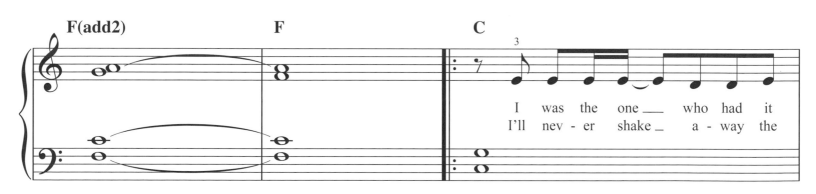

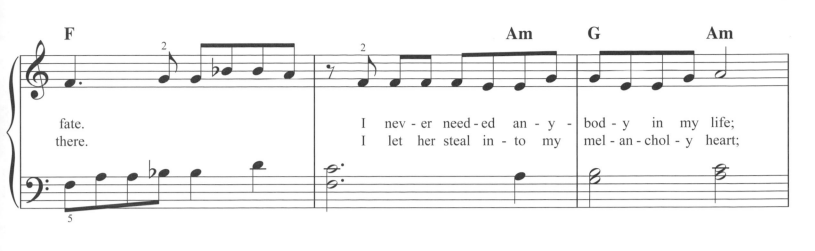

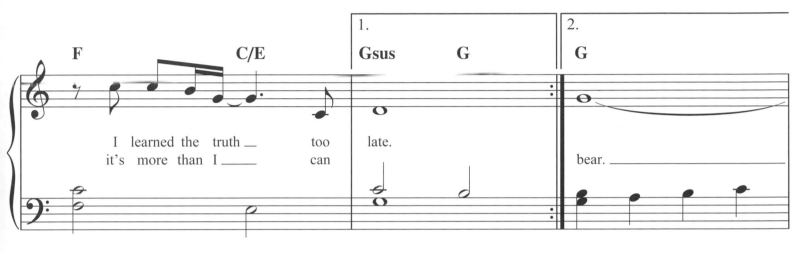

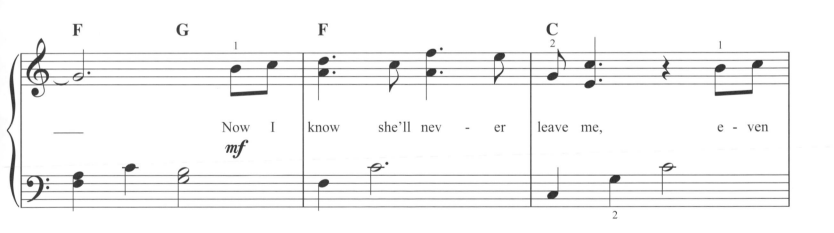

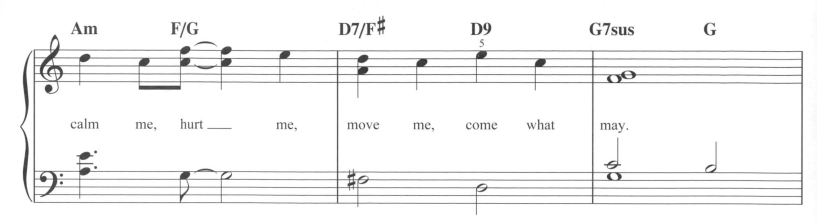

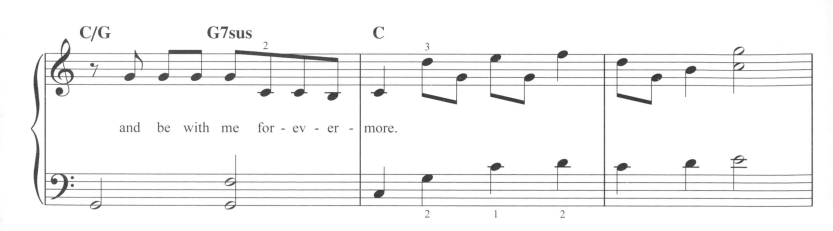

I rage a-gainst __ the trials of love. I curse the fad-ing of the

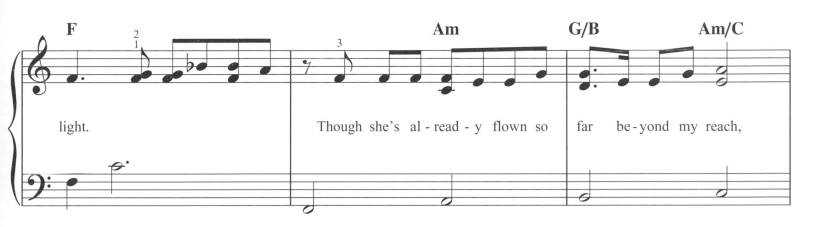

light. Though she's al-read-y flown so far be-yond my reach,

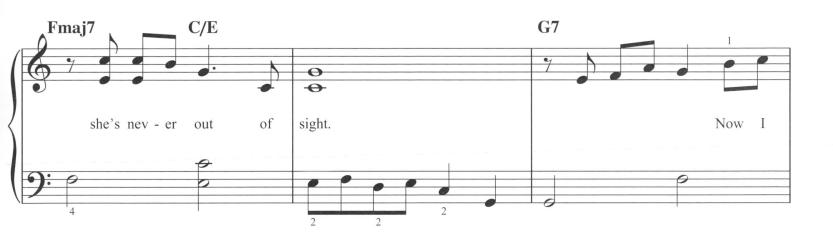

she's nev-er out of sight. Now I

know she'll nev - er leave me, e - ven as she fades from

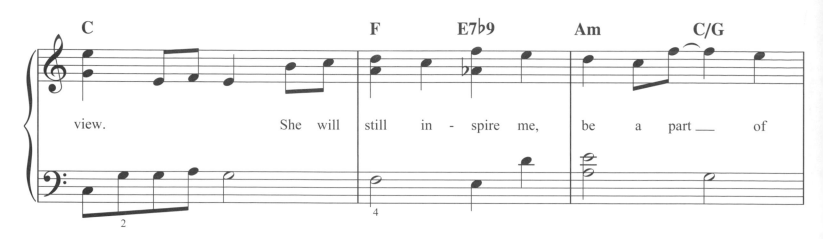

view. She will still in - spire me, be a part ___ of

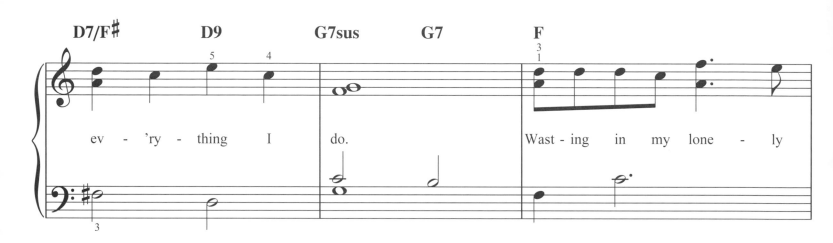

ev - 'ry - thing I do. Wast - ing in my lone - ly

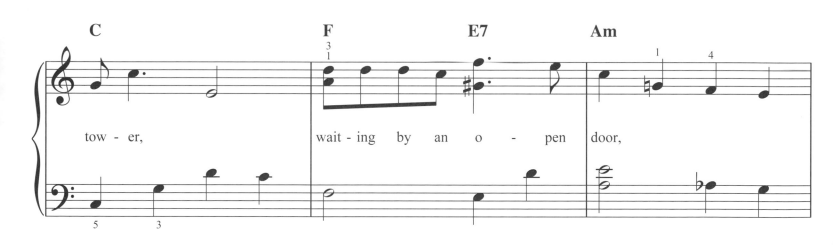

tow - er, wait - ing by an o - pen door,

I'll fool my - self she'll walk right in,

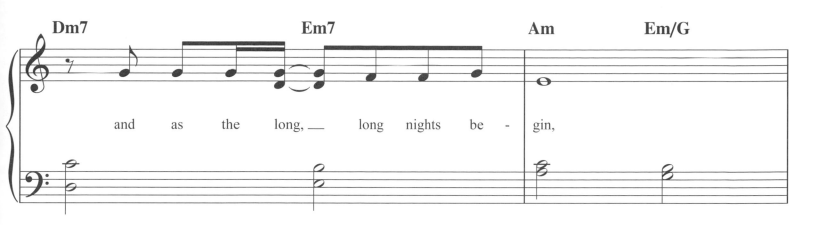

and as the long, ___ long nights be - gin,

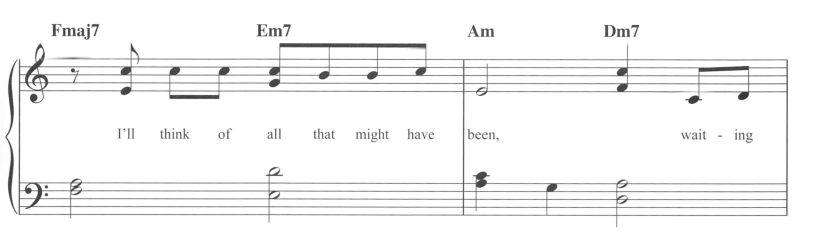

I'll think of all that might have been, wait - ing

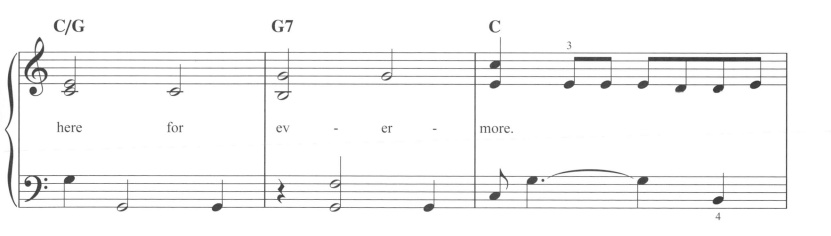

here for ev - er - more.

HOW DOES A MOMENT LAST FOREVER

(As performed by Celine Dion)
from BEAUTY AND THE BEAST

Music by ALAN MENKEN
Lyrics by TIM RICE

Gently

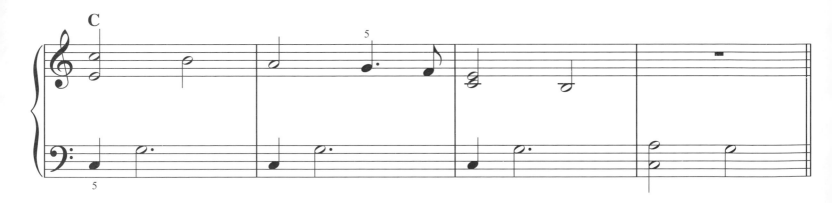

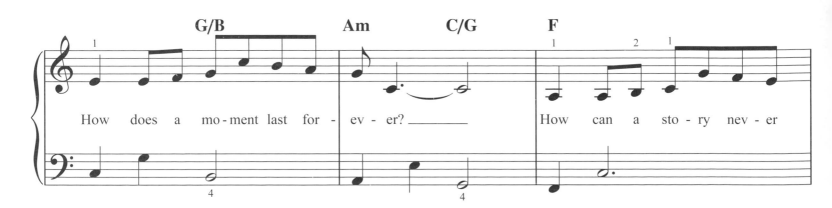

How does a mo-ment last for-ev-er? _____ How can a sto-ry nev-er

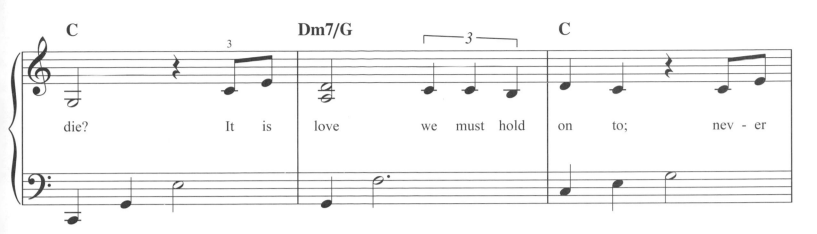

die? It is love we must hold on to; nev - er

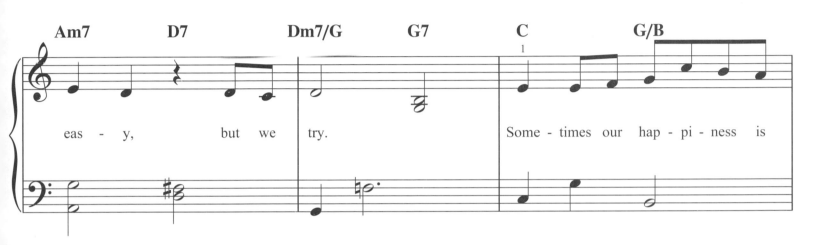

eas - y, but we try. Some - times our hap - pi - ness is

cap - tured; _____ some - how, a time and place stand still.

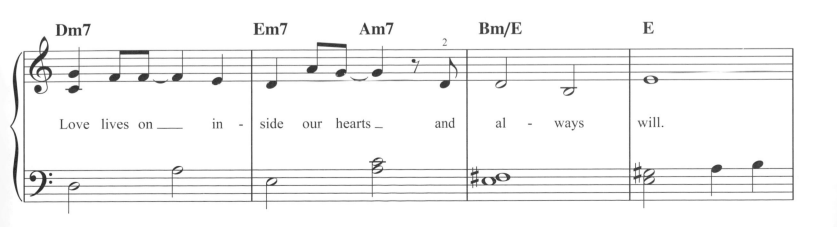

Love lives on ___ in - side our hearts _ and al - ways will.

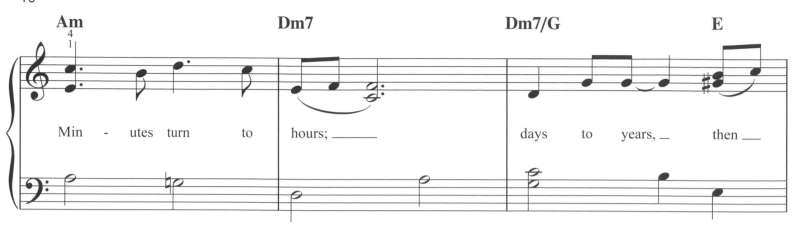

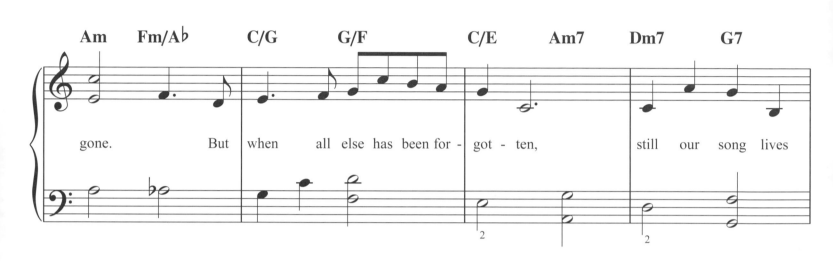

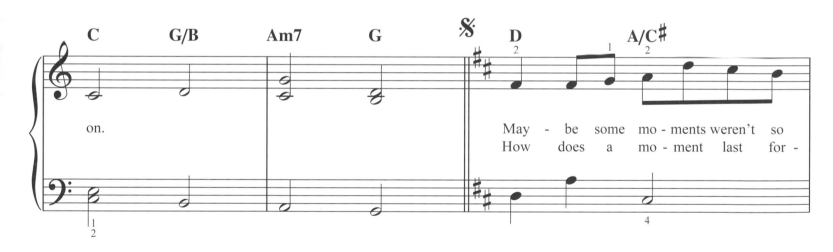

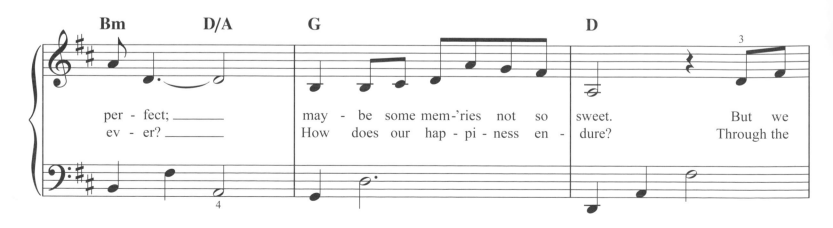

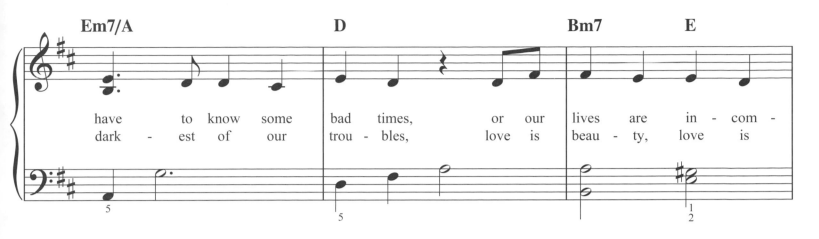

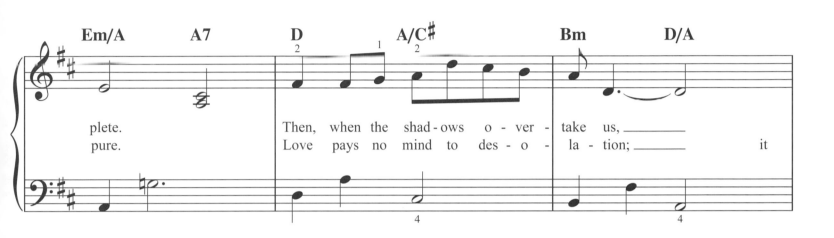

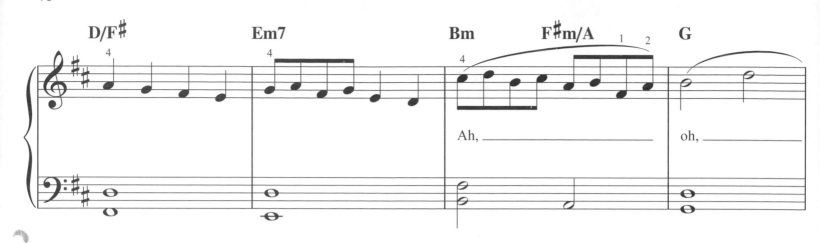

Ah, _____ oh, _____

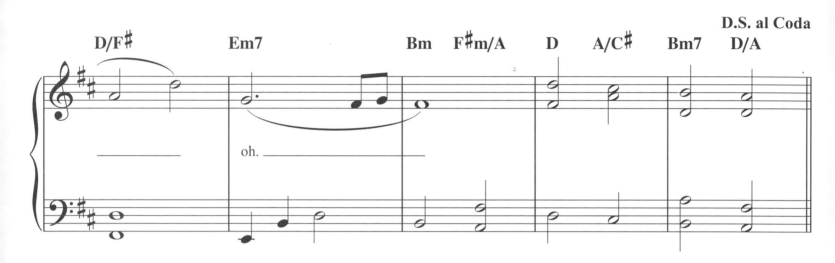

D.S. al Coda

_____ oh. _____

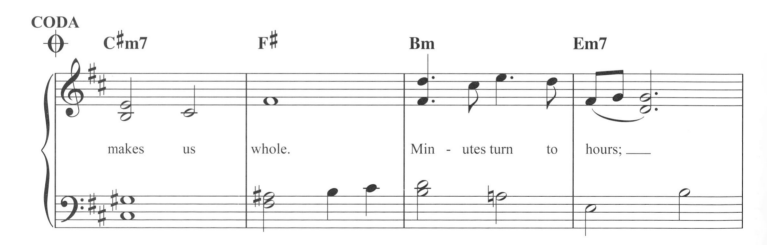

CODA

makes us whole. Min - utes turn to hours; ___

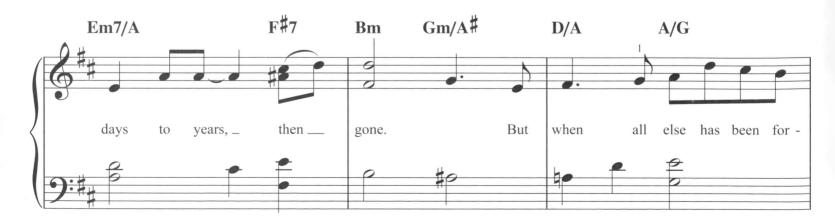

days to years, _ then ___ gone. But when all else has been for -

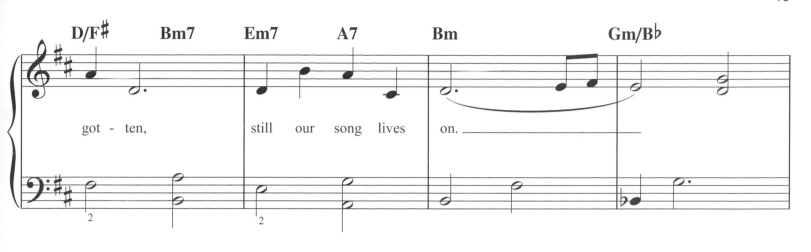

got - ten,   still   our song lives   on. _____

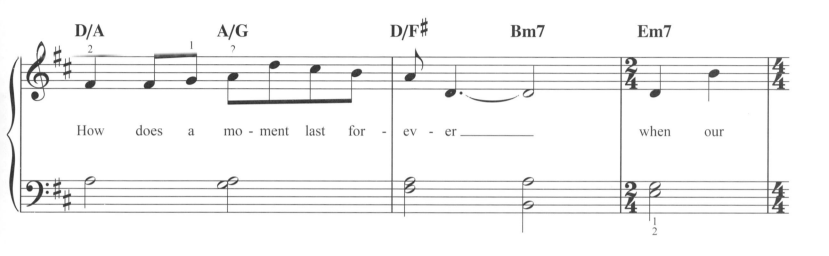

How   does a   mo - ment last for - ev - er _____ when our

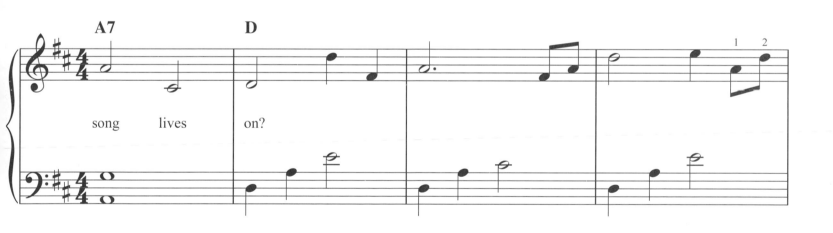

song   lives   on?

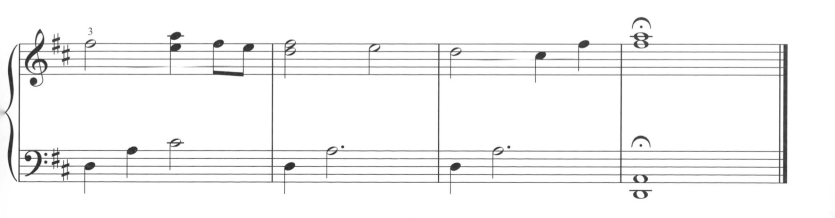

BEAUTY AND THE BEAST

from BEAUTY AND THE BEAST

Music by ALAN MENKEN
Lyrics by HOWARD ASHMAN

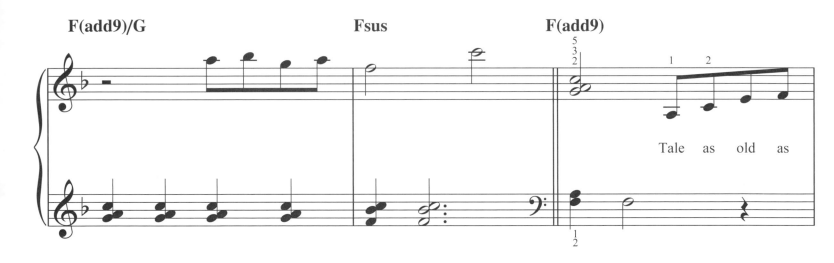

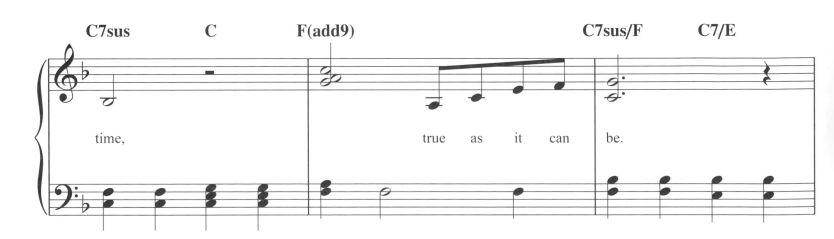

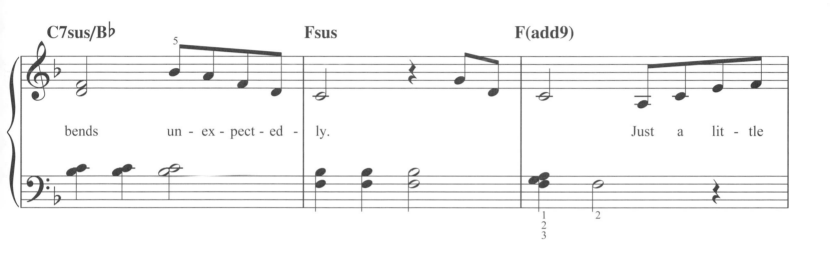

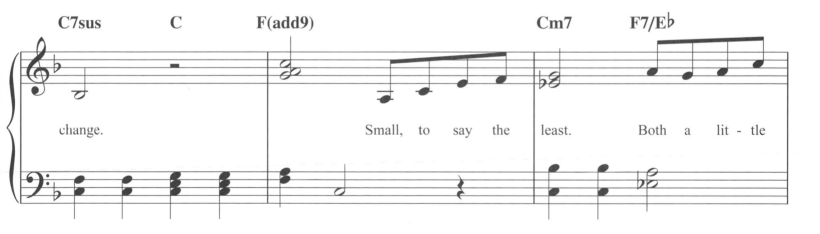

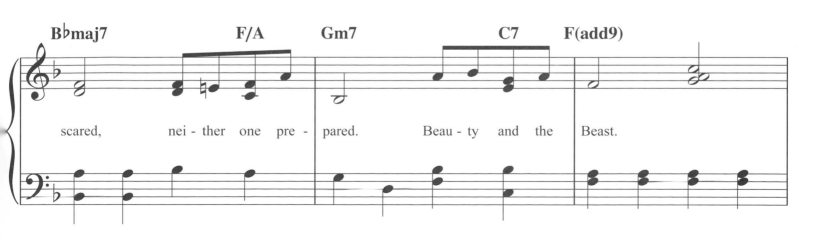

Ev - er just the same. Ev - er a sur-

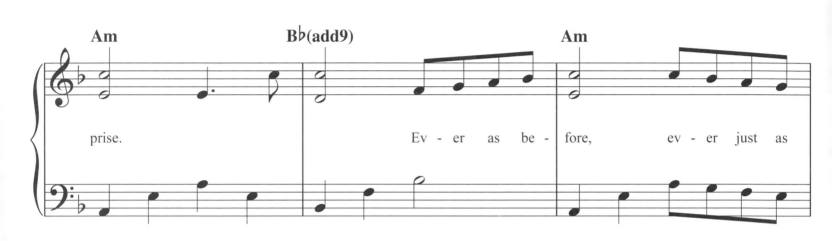

prise. Ev - er as be - fore, ev - er just as

sure as the sun will rise. Tale as old as

time. Tune as old as song.

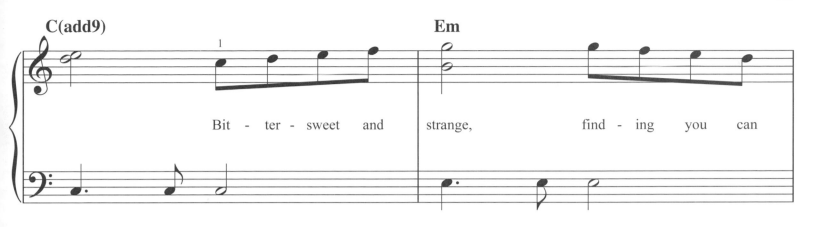

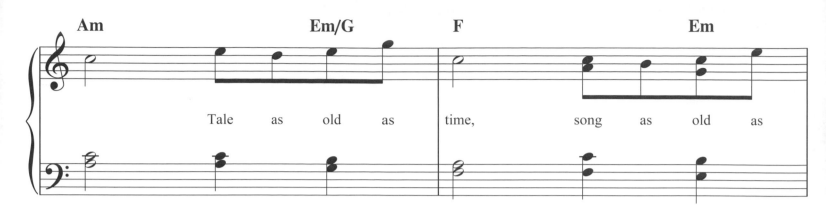

Tale as old as time, song as old as

rhyme. Beau - ty and the Beast.

a tempo

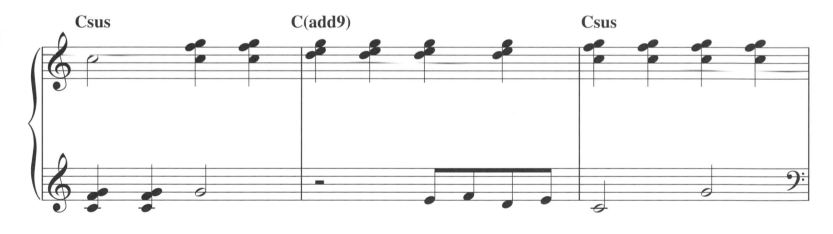

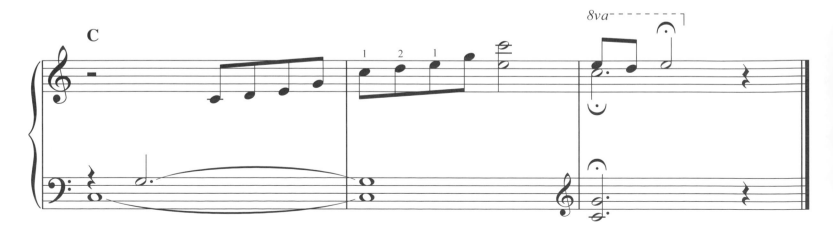

THE WORLD ES MI FAMILIA

from COCO

Music by GERMAINE FRANCO
Lyrics by ADRIAN MOLINA

Moderately fast, in 2

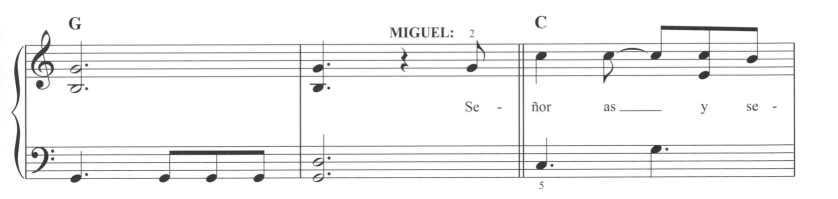

ñor - es. To be here with you to - night _____ brings me

joy! Que al - e - grí - a! ____ For this mu - sic is my

lan - guage and the world es ____ mi fa - mi - lia. ____

For this mu - sic is my

lan - guage __ and the world es mi fa - mi - lia. __

ERNESTO DE LA CRUZ & MIGUEL:

For this mu - sic __ is my lan - guage __ and the

world __ es __ mi fa - mi - lia. __

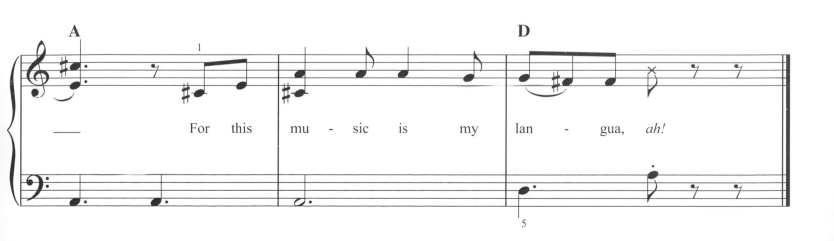

For this mu - sic is my lan - gua, *ah!*

REMEMBER ME

(Ernesto de la Cruz)
from COCO

Words and Music by KRISTEN ANDERSON-LOPEZ
and ROBERT LOPEZ

Moderately fast

ERNESTO DE LA CRUZ:

Re - mem - ber me, though I have to say good- bye. Re - mem - ber me, don't let it make you cry. For e - ven if I'm far a - way, __ I hold you in my heart. I sing a se - cret song to you each

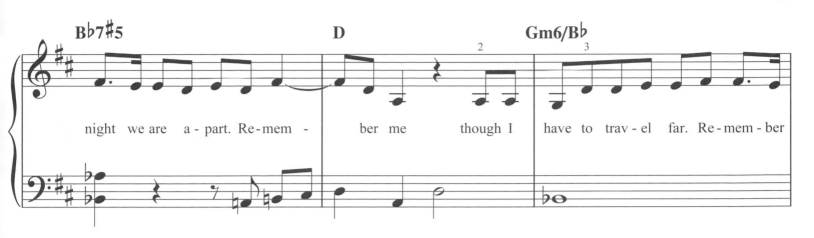

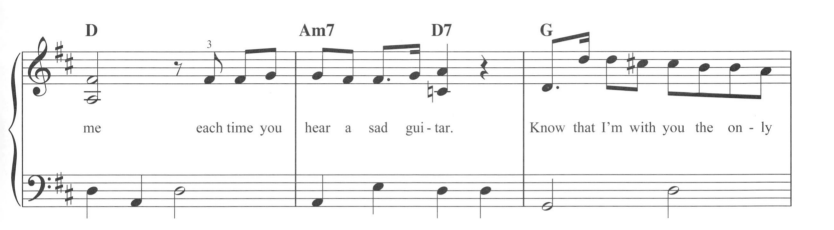

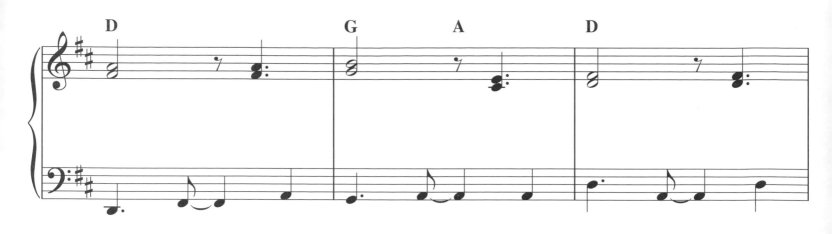

Re - mem - ber

me,   though I   have to   say good- bye. Re - mem - ber   me,   don't

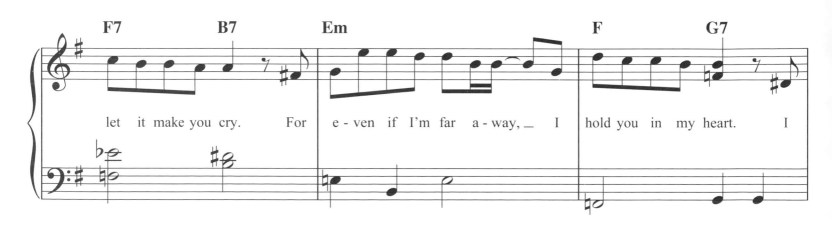

let it make you cry.   For   e - ven if I'm far a - way, _ I   hold you   in   my heart.   I

sing a se-cret song to you each night we are a-part. Re-mem - ber me though I

have to trav-el far. Re-mem-ber me each time you hear a sad gui-tar.

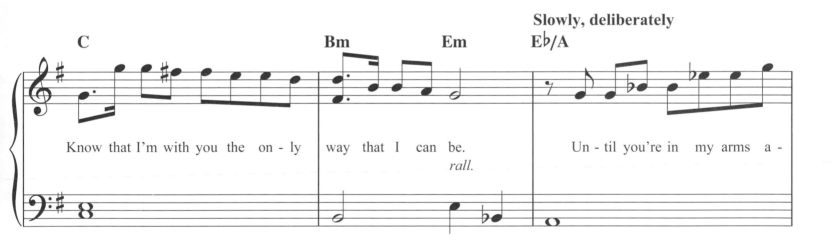

Know that I'm with you the on-ly way that I can be. *rall.* Un-til you're in my arms a-

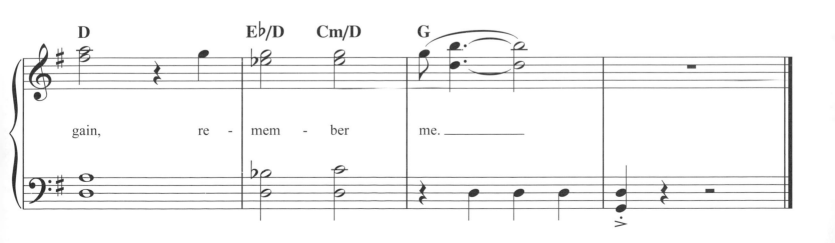

gain, re - mem - ber me.

UN POCO LOCO

from COCO

Music by GERMAINE FRANCO
Lyrics by ADRIAN MOLINA

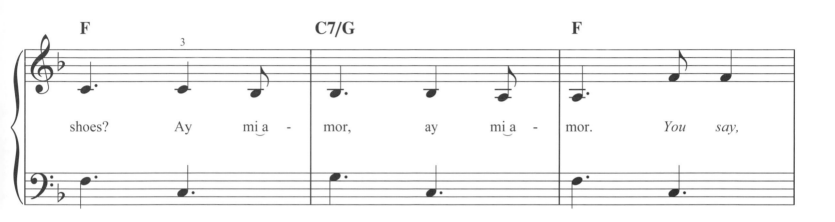

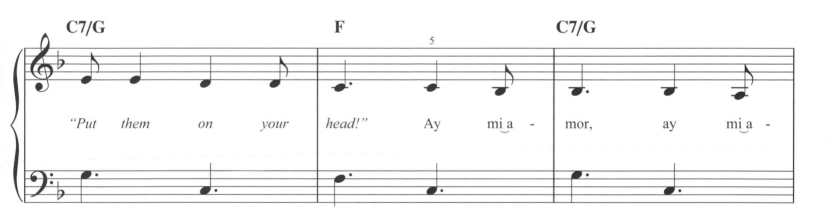

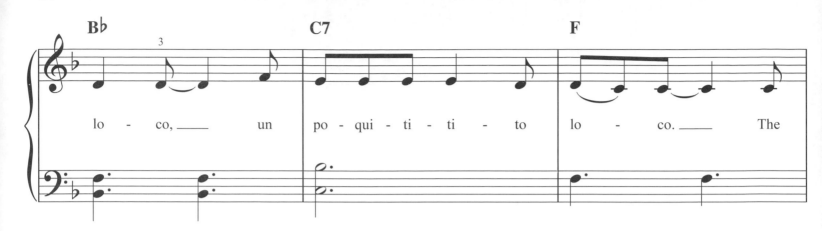

lo - co, _____ un po - qui - ti - ti - to lo - co. _____ The

way you keep me guess - ing, I'm _____ nod - ding and I'm

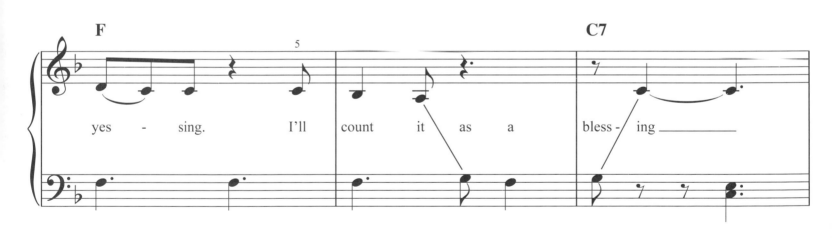

yes - sing. I'll count it as a bless - ing _____

that I'm on - ly _____ un po - co

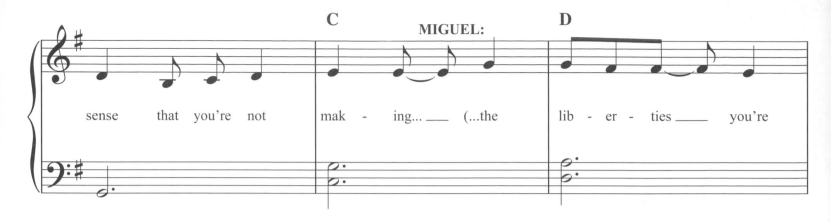

sense that you're not **mak - ing...** (...the **lib - er - ties** you're

tak - ing...) leaves my ca - be - za shak - ing.

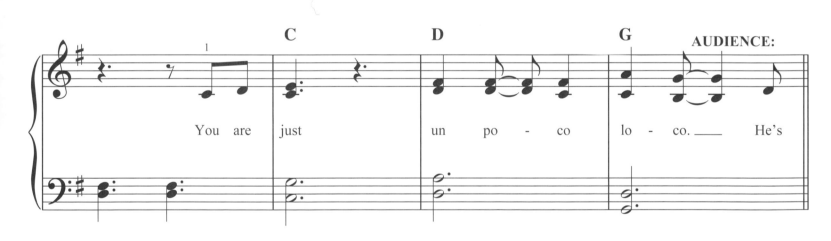

You are just un po - co lo - co. He's

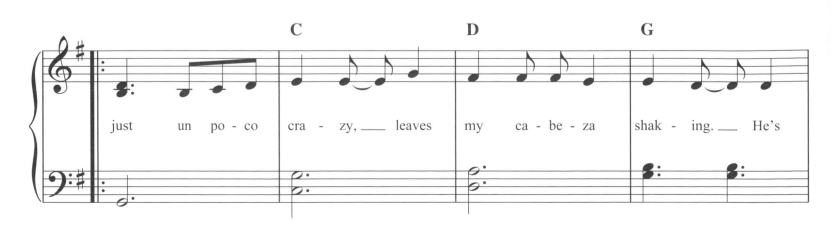

just un po - co cra - zy, leaves my ca - be - za shak - ing. He's

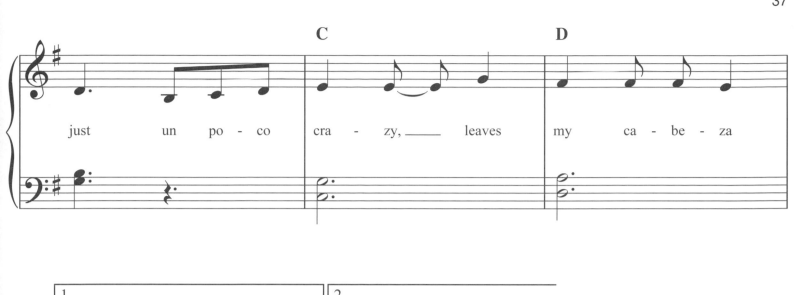

just un po - co cra - zy, ___ leaves my ca - be - za

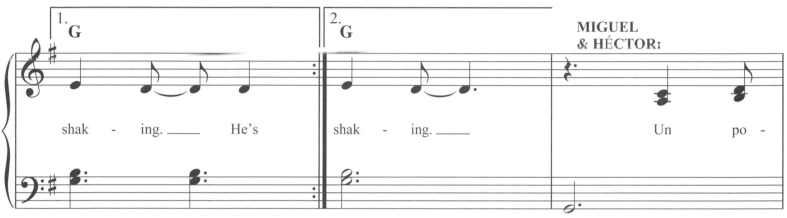

1. **G** shak - ing. ___ He's
2. **G** shak - ing. ___

MIGUEL
& HÉCTOR:

Un po -

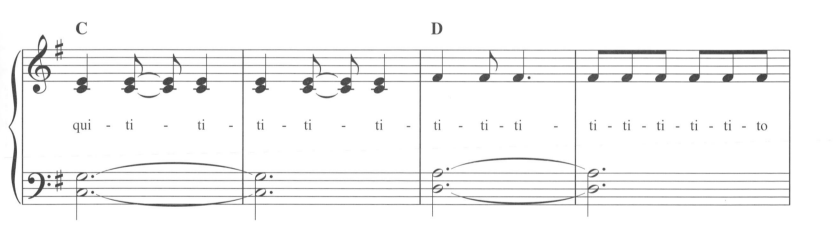

C **D**

qui - ti - ti - ti - ti - ti - ti - ti - ti - ti - ti - ti - ti - ti - to

G **Gsus** **G**

lo - co. ___

DO YOU WANT TO BUILD A SNOWMAN?

from FROZEN

Music and Lyrics by KRISTEN ANDERSON-LOPEZ
and ROBERT LOPEZ

Moderately fast

LITTLE ANNA: *(Spoken:)* Elsa? (knocks)   *(Sung:)* Do you want to build a   snow - man?

Come on, let's go and   play!   I nev - er see you

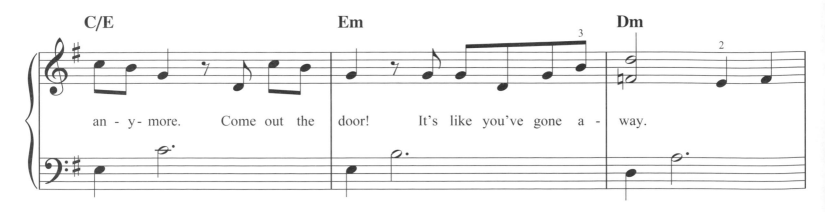

an - y - more.   Come out the   door!   It's like you've gone a - way.

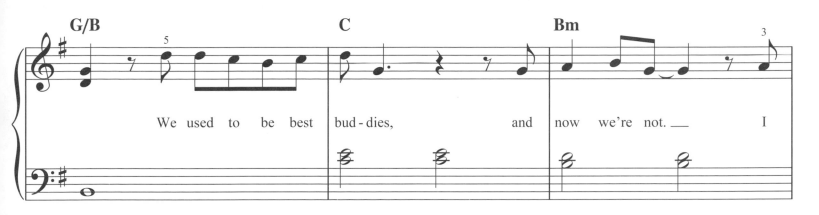

We used to be best bud-dies, and now we're not. ___ I

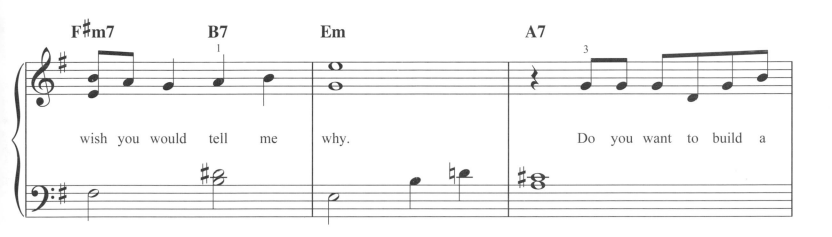

wish you would tell me why. Do you want to build a

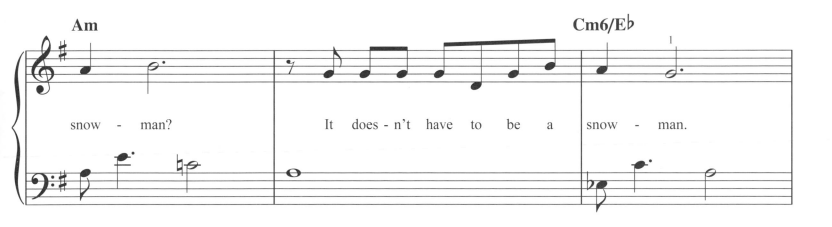

snow-man? It does-n't have to be a snow-man.

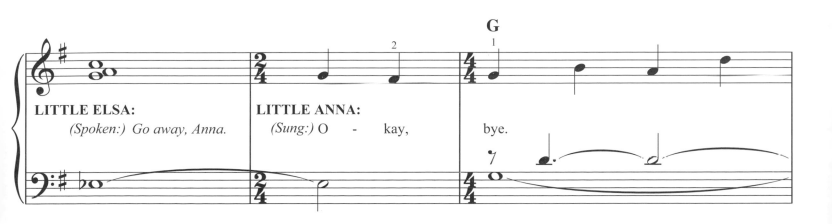

LITTLE ELSA:
(Spoken:) Go away, Anna.

LITTLE ANNA:
(Sung:) O - kay, bye.

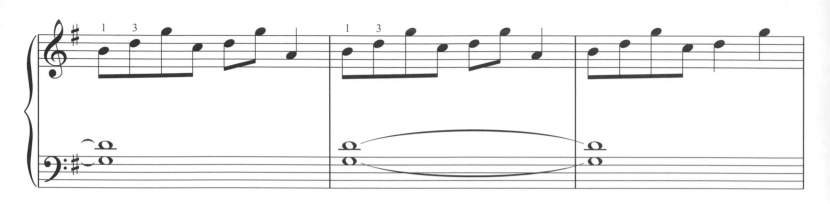

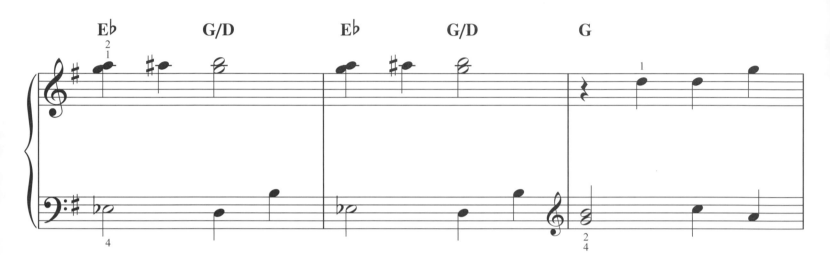

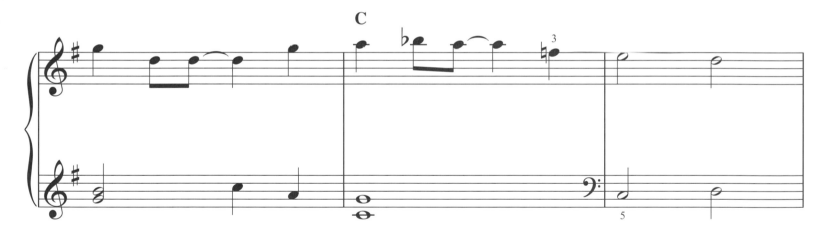

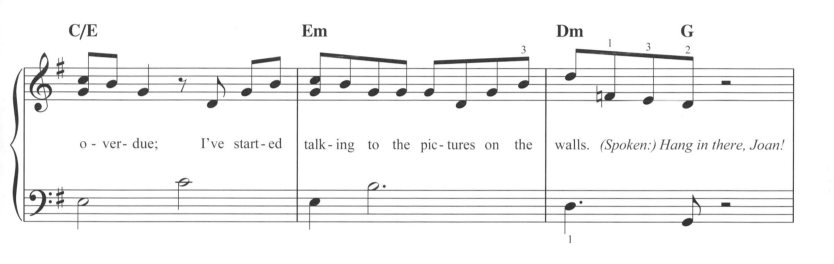

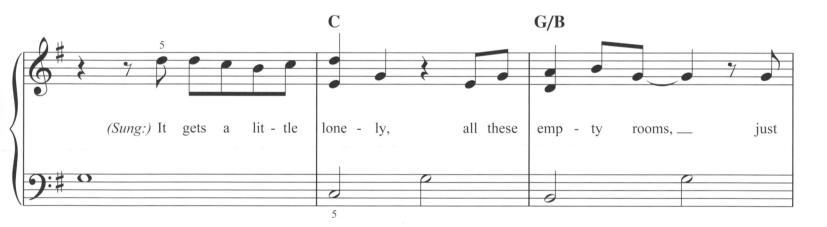

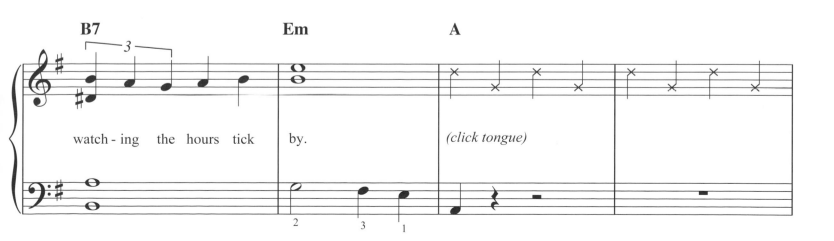

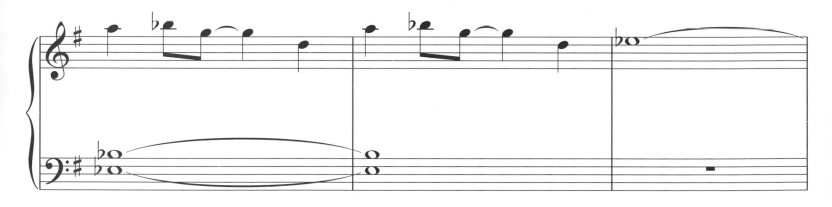

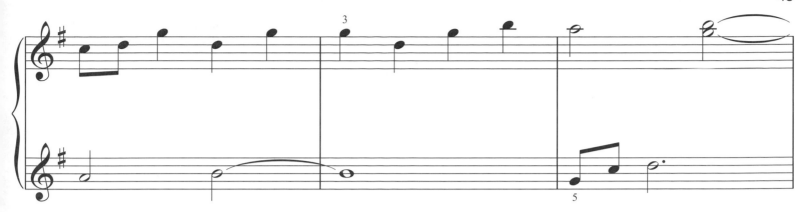

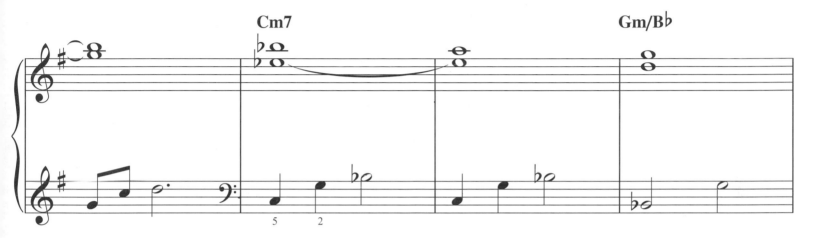

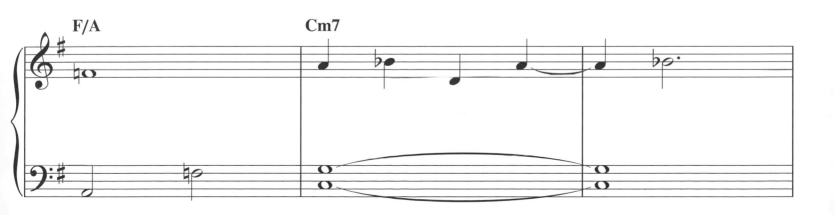

44

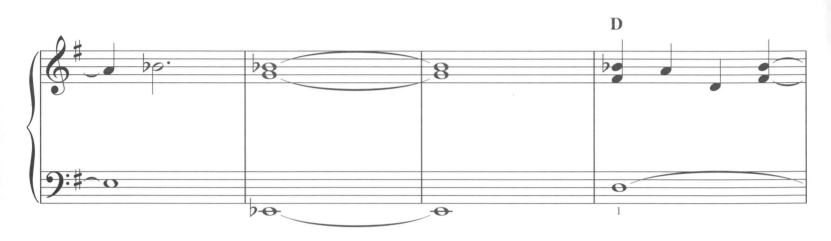

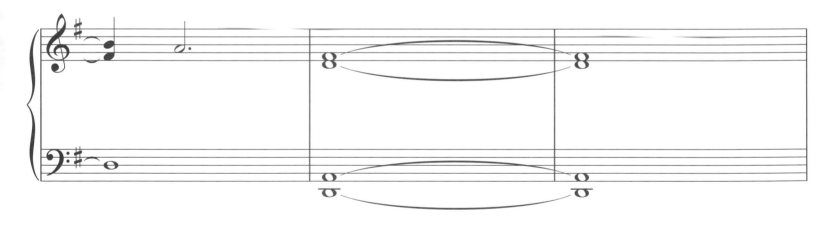

Slower, tenderly

(knocking) *(Spoken:)* Elsa? *(Sung:)* Please, I know you're in there.

Peo - ple are ask-ing where you've been. They say, "Have cour - age," and I'm

try - ing to; I'm right out here for you, just let me in.

We on - ly have each oth - er; it's just you and me.

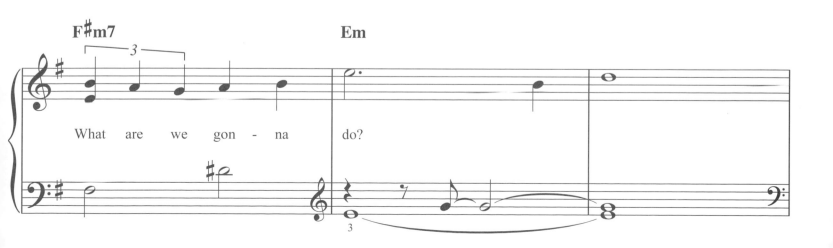

What are we gon - na do?

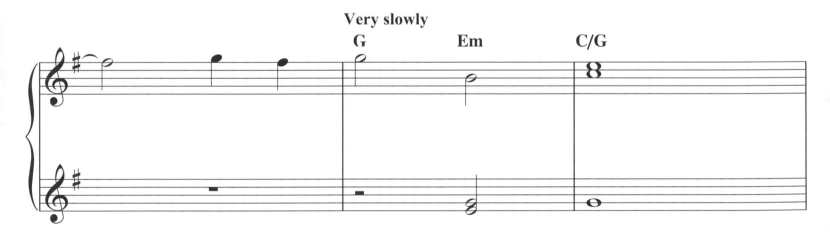

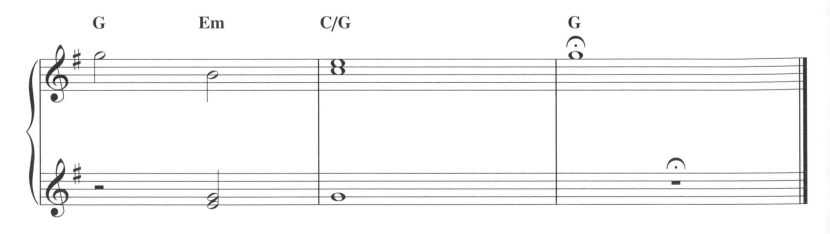

LET IT GO
from FROZEN

Music and Lyrics by KRISTEN ANDERSON-LOPEZ
and ROBERT LOPEZ

Half-time feel, mysterious

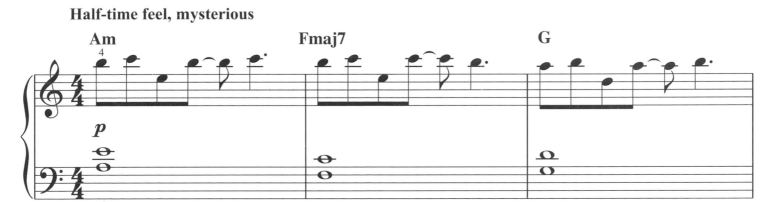

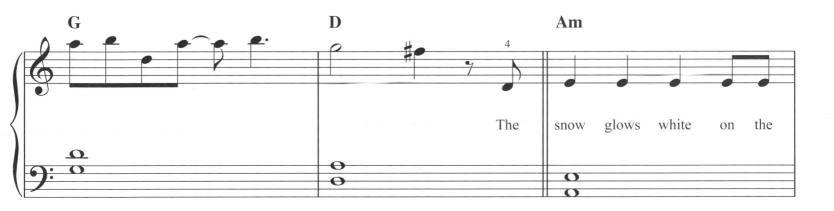

The snow glows white on the

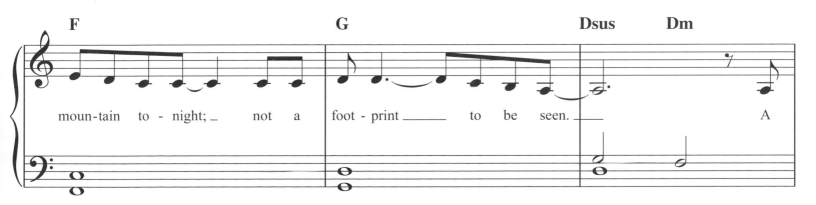

moun-tain to-night;__ not a foot-print ____ to be seen. ____ A

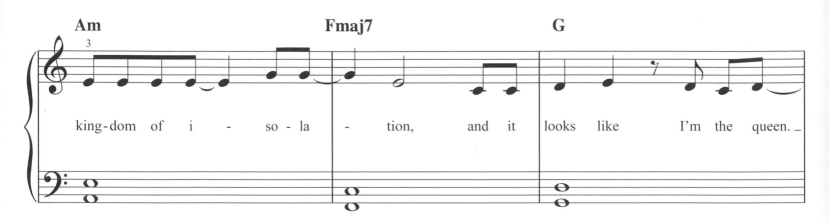

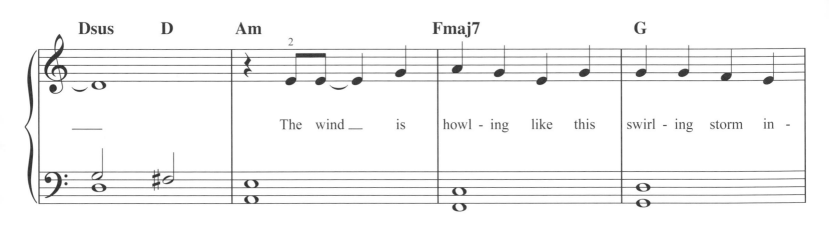

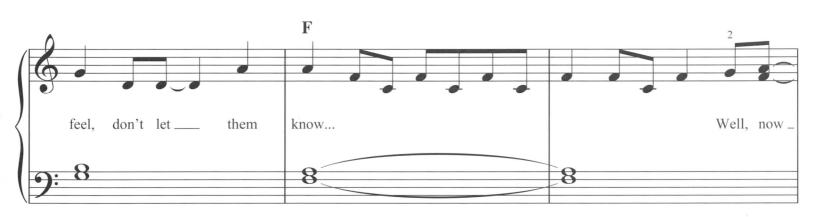

let it go; _____ turn a - way _____ and slam _____ the _____
let it go; _____ you'll nev - er see _____ me _____

door. _____ I don't _____ care _____ what they're
cry. _____ Here I _____ stand, _____ and

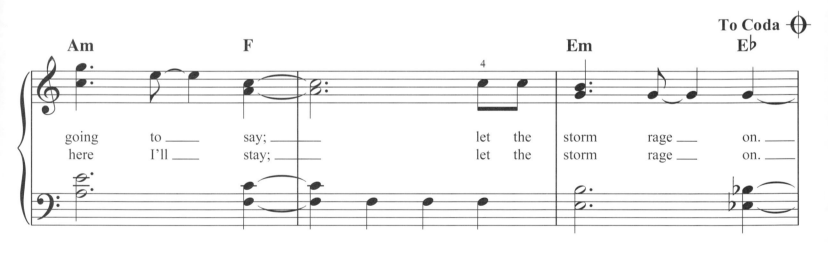

going to _____ say; _____ let the storm rage _____ on.
here I'll _____ stay; _____ let the storm rage _____ on. _____

To Coda

The cold nev - er both - ered me an - y - way.

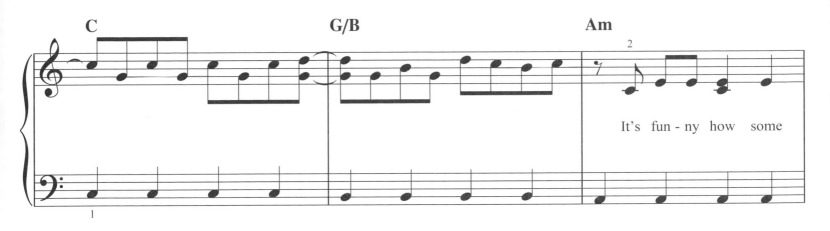

C **G/B** **Am**

It's fun - ny how some

F **G** **Dm**

dis - tance makes ev - 'ry - thing __ seem small; and the

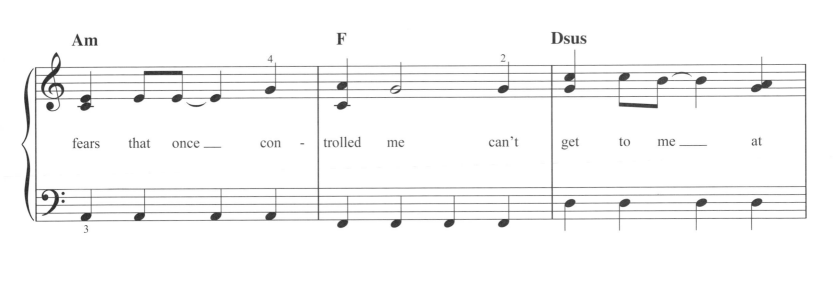

Am **F** **Dsus**

fears that once __ con - trolled me can't get to me __ at

D **G**

all. It's time __ to see what I can

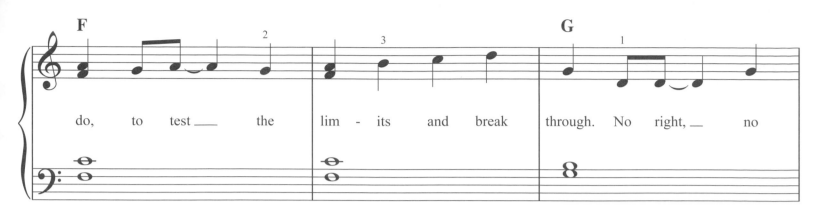

do, to test ___ the lim - its and break through. No right, ___ no

wrong, no rules for me, ___ I'm free!

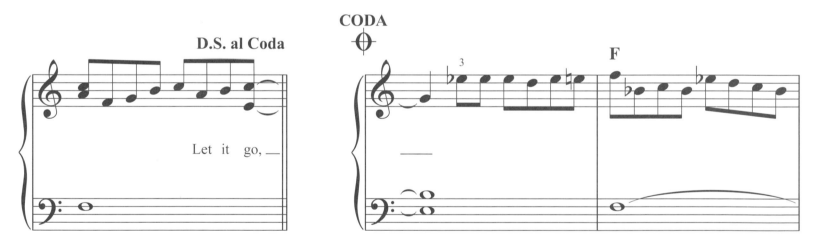

D.S. al Coda

Let it go, ___

CODA

___

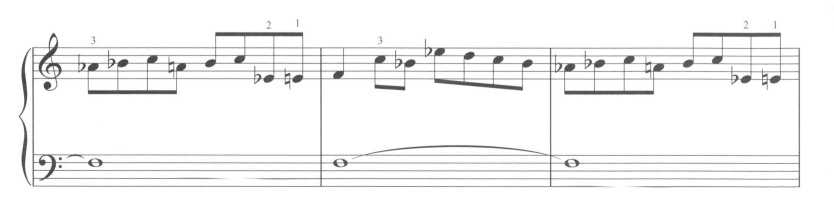

My pow - er flur - ries through the air in - to the

ground. My soul __ is spi - ral - ing in

fro - zen frac - tals all a - round. __ And one __ thought

cry - stal - liz - es like an i - cy blast:

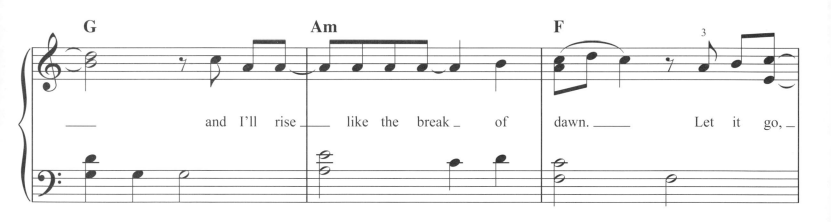

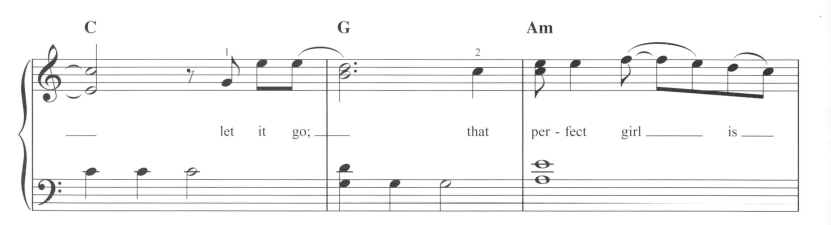

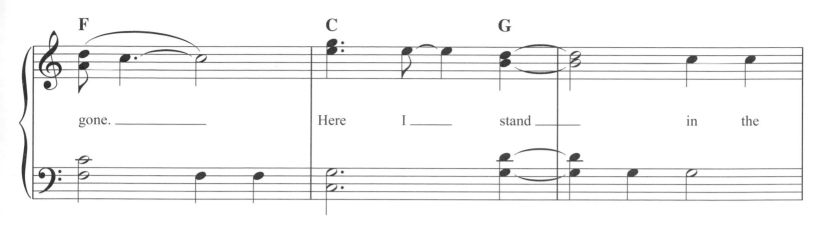

F

gone. _____

C

Here I ____ stand ____ in the

G

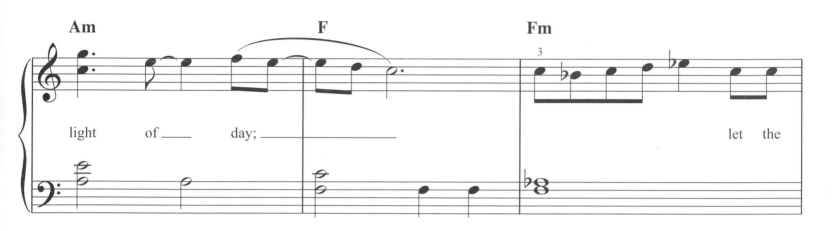

Am

light of ____ day; _____

F

Fm

3

let the

Em

storm rage ____ on. _____

Eb

4

The

F

cold nev - er both - ered me an - y - way. _____

LAVA
from LAVA

Music and Lyrics by
JAMES FORD MURPHY

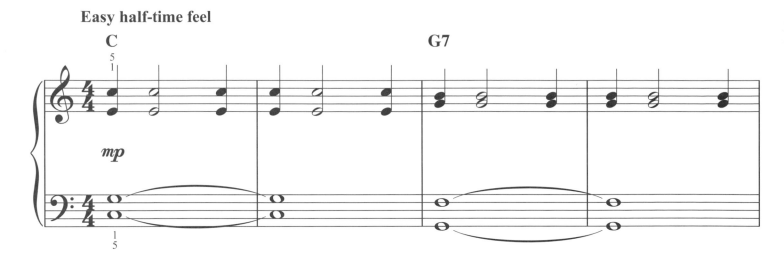

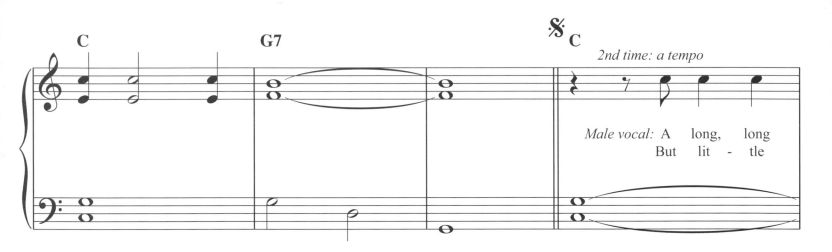

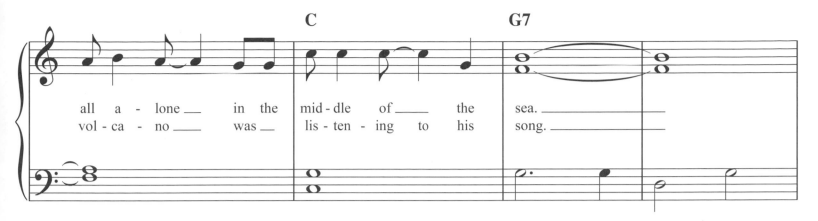

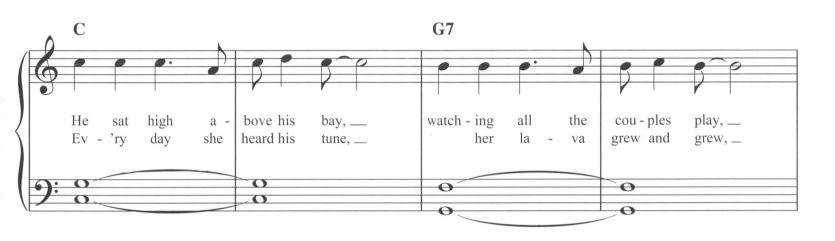

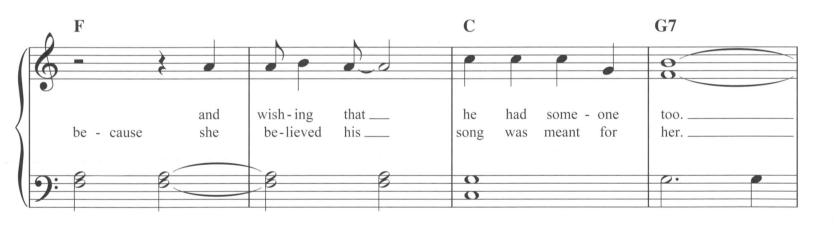

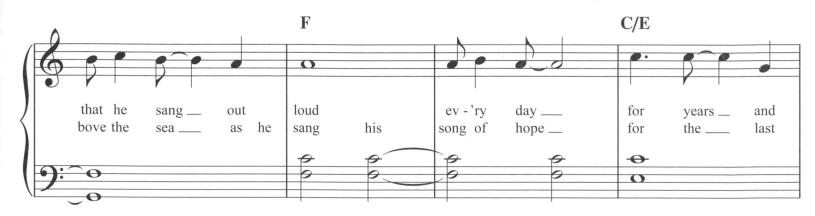

that he sang ___ out loud ev -'ry day ___ for years ___ and
bove the sea ___ as he sang his song of hope ___ for the ___ last

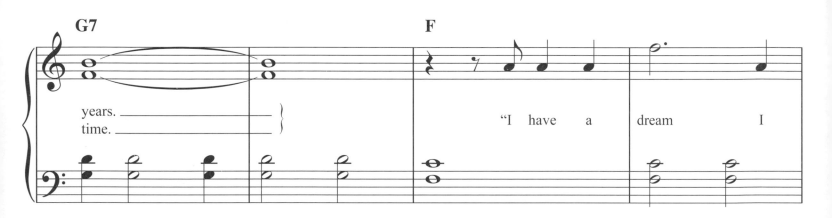

years. _____
time. _____

"I have a dream I

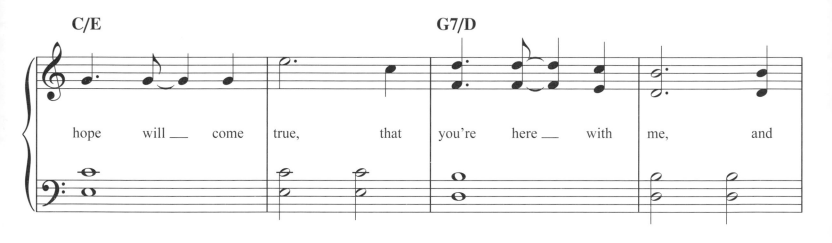

hope will ___ come true, that you're here ___ with me, and

I'm here ___ with you. I wish that ___ the earth, sea, ___ and the

To Coda

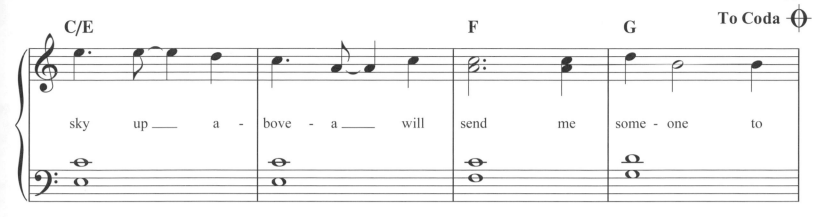

Slower

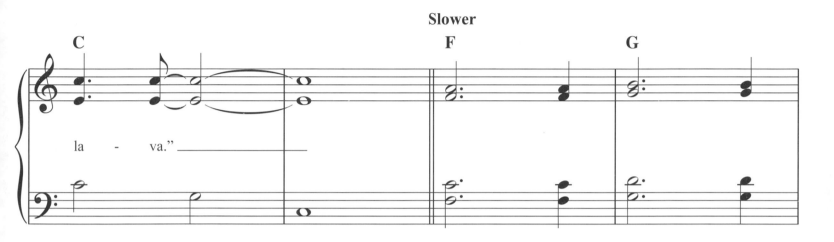

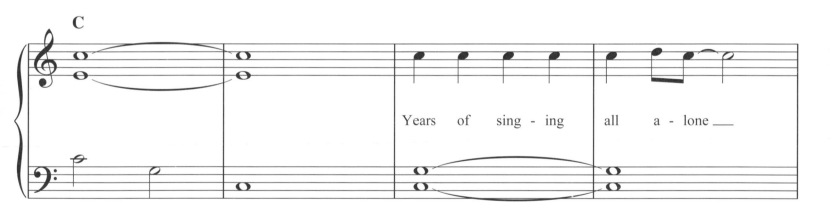

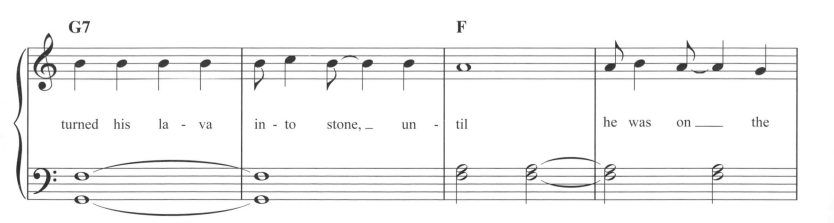

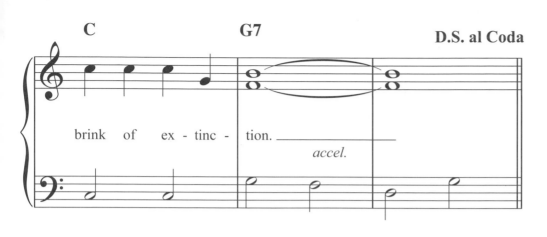

brink of ex - tinc - tion. _____ *accel.*

CODA

la - va." _____

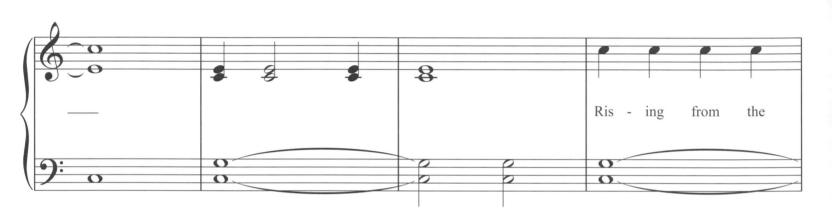

Ris - ing from the

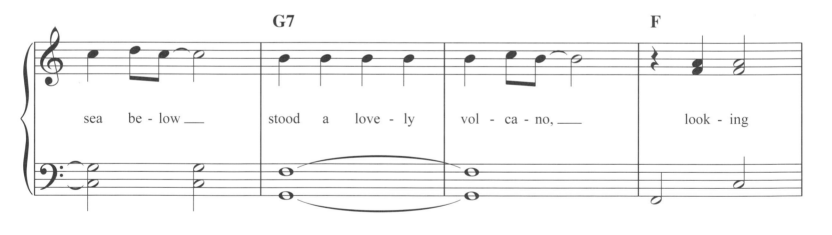

sea be - low ___ stood a love - ly vol - ca - no, ___ look - ing

all a - round, _ but she could not ___ see him. _____ He

tried to sing to / let her know ___ that / she was not / there a - lone, ___ but
filled the sea ___ / with his tears, ___ and / watched his dreams / dis - ap - pear ___ as

with no ___ / la - va his ___ / song was ___ all / gone. ___
she re - / mem - bered what ___ his / song meant ___ to /

1.

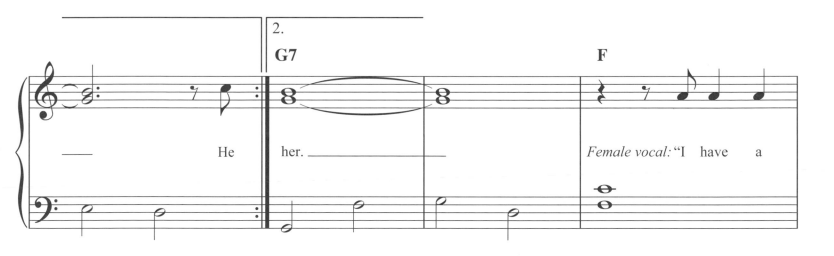

___ He / her. ___ / *Female vocal:* "I have a

2.

dream I / hope will ___ come / true, that / you're here ___ with

me,   and   I'm   here __ with   you.   I   wish that __ the

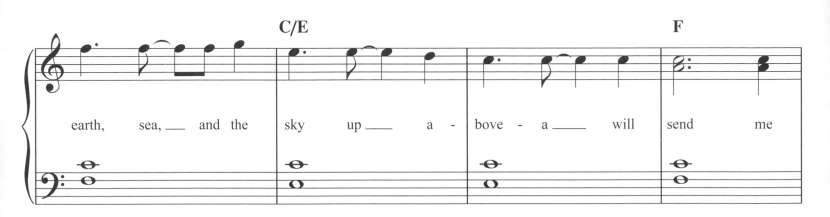

earth,   sea, __ and the   sky   up __ a - bove - a __ will   send   me

some - one   to   la - va." _____

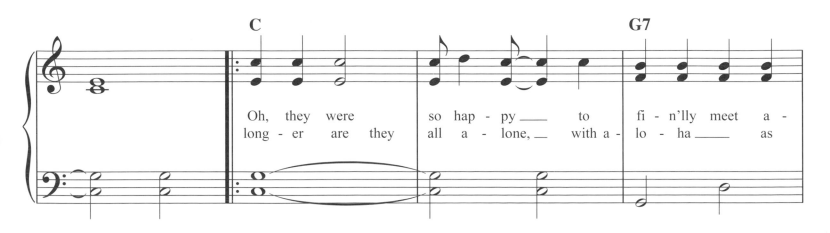

Oh,   they   were   so hap - py __ to   fi - n'lly meet a -
long - er   are they   all a - lone, __ with a - lo - ha __ as

bove the sea. ___   All ___ to - geth - er now ___ their   la - va grew and
their new home, ___   and when you vis - it them ___   this is what they

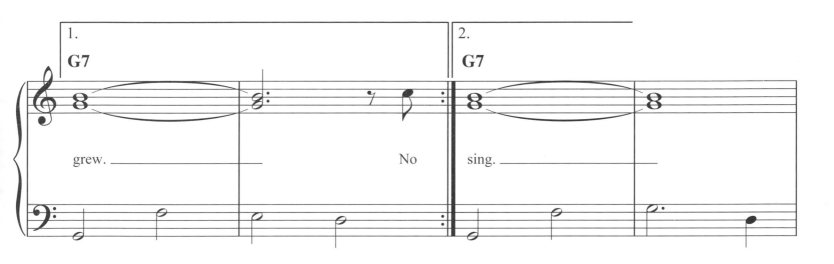

grew. ___   No   sing. ___

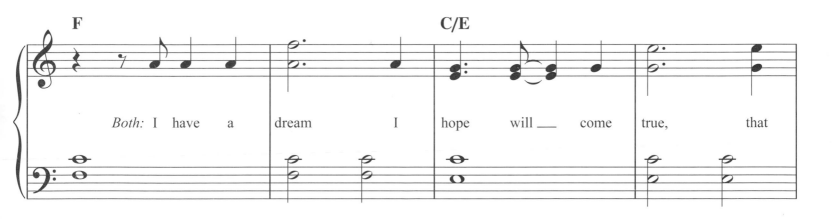

Both: I have a   dream I hope will ___ come true, that

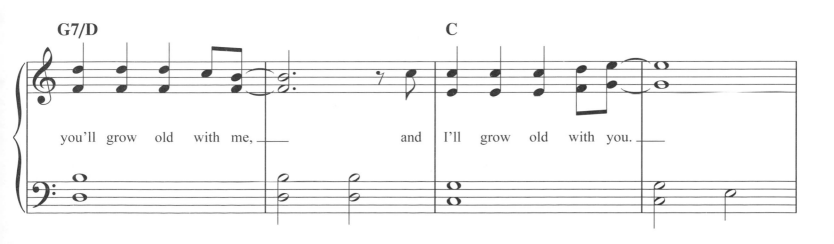

you'll grow old with me, ___   and I'll grow old with you. ___

We thank ___ you earth, sea, ___ and the sky we ___ thank too,

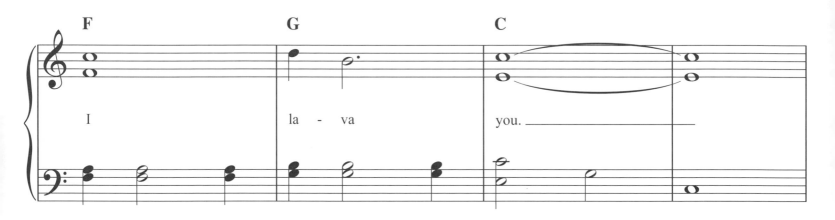

I la - va you. ___

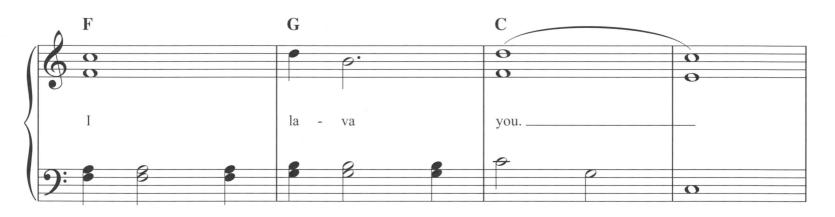

I la - va you. ___

A little slower

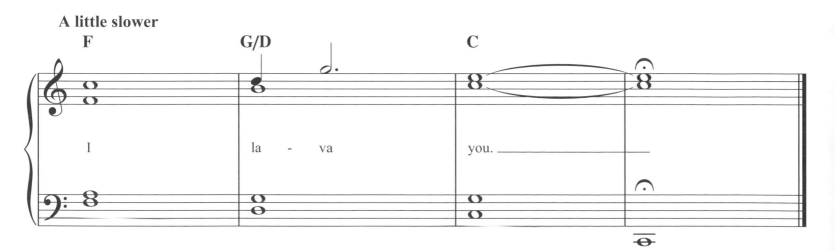

I la - va you. ___

HOW FAR I'LL GO
from MOANA

Music and Lyrics by
LIN-MANUEL MIRANDA

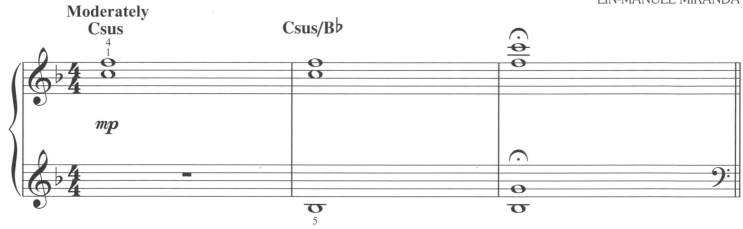

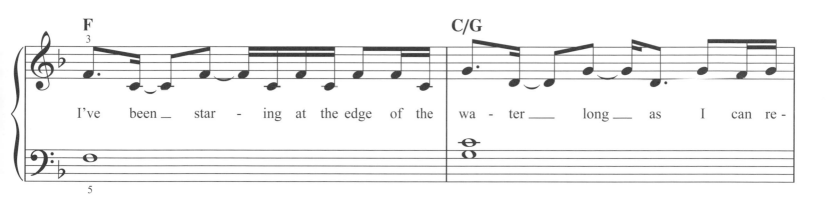

I've been __ star - ing at the edge of the wa - ter __ long __ as I can re-

mem - ber, __ nev - er real - ly know - ing why. I wish __ I could be the per - fect

daugh - ter, __ but I come back to the wa - ter __ no mat - ter how hard I try. Ev - 'ry

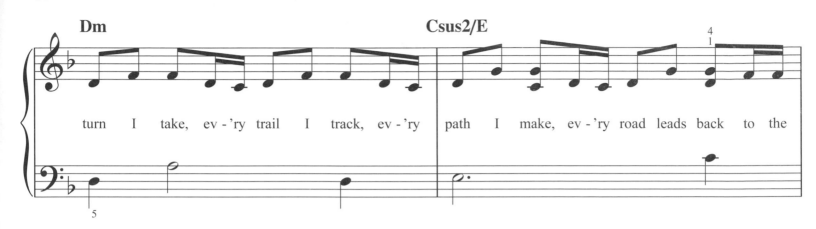

turn I take, ev-'ry trail I track, ev-'ry path I make, ev-'ry road leads back to the

place I know where I can-not go, where I long _____ to be. See the

line where the sky meets the sea, it calls _____ me, and no one knows _____ how far it

goes. _____ If the wind in my sail on the sea stays be-hind _____ me, one day I'll

Dm7   **B♭m6**   **F**

know. _____ If I | go, there's just no tell-ing how far I'll | go. I ___ know _ ev-'ry-bod-y on this

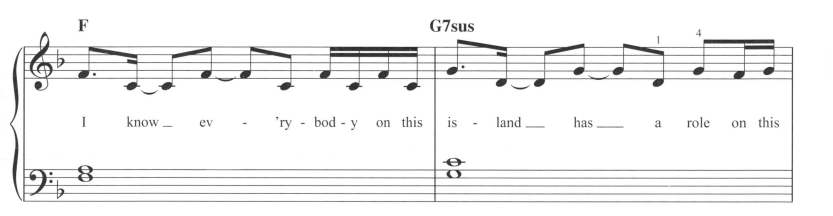

G7sus   **Dm**   **B♭sus2**

is - land ___ seems _ so hap-py on this | is - land. _ Ev'ry-thing is by de-sign. ___

F   **G7sus**

I know ___ ev - 'ry - bod - y on this | is - land ___ has ___ a role on this

Dm   **B♭**

is - land, ___ so may-be I can roll with mine. ___ | I can

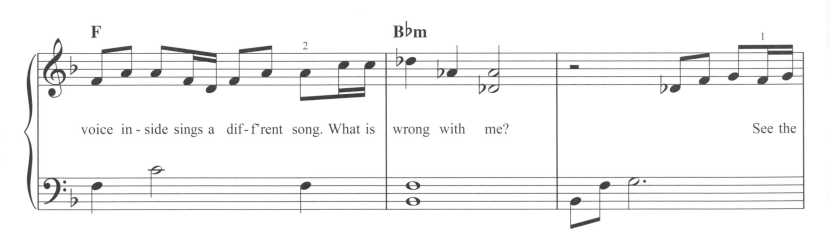

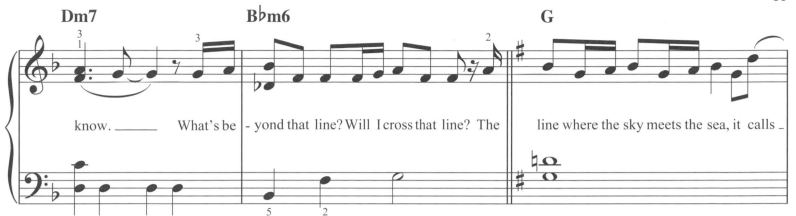

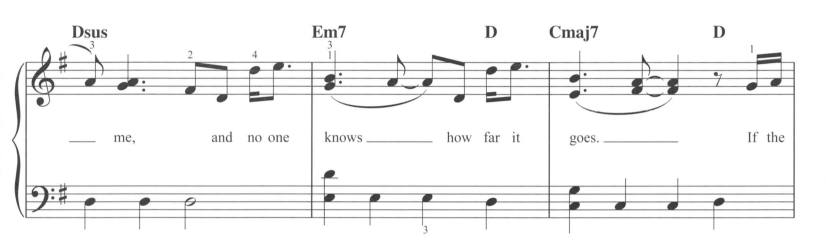

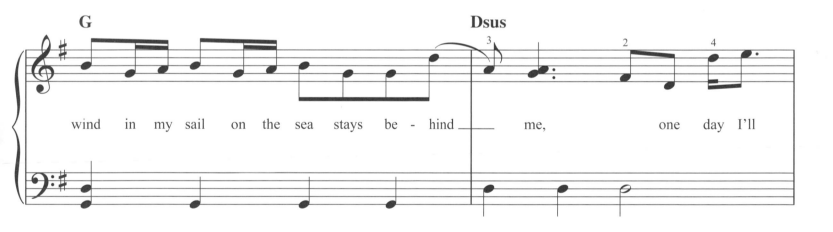

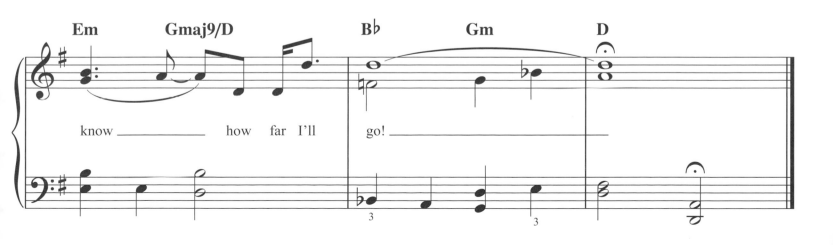

WE KNOW THE WAY

from MOANA

Music by OPETAIA FOA'I
Lyrics by OPETAIA FOA'I
and LIN-MANUEL MIRANDA

Moderately

Ta - tou ta - ga - ta fo - lau va - la - 'a ui - na

e le a - tu - a. O le sa - mi te - le _____ e o mai

la a - va - 'e le lu - 'i tau e - le - lei. _____ Ta - pe - na - pe - na _____

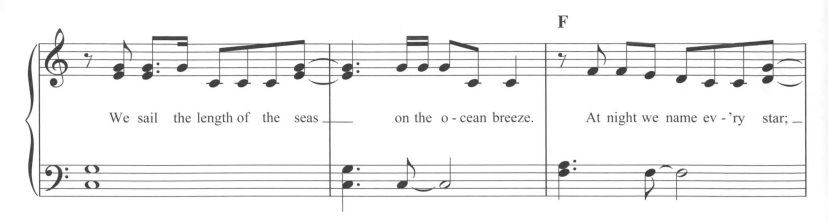

and when it's time to find home, we know the way. A - way, a - way. We are ex -

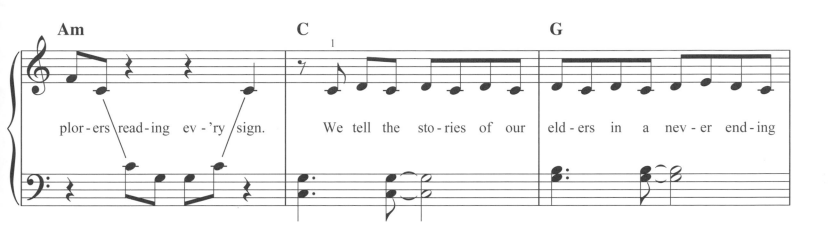

plor - ers read - ing ev - 'ry sign. We tell the sto - ries of our eld - ers in a nev - er end - ing

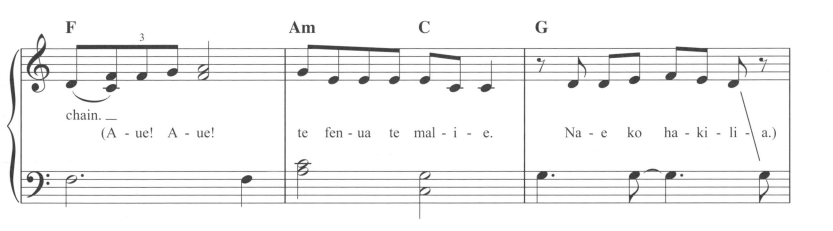

chain. ___ (A - ue! A - ue! te fen - ua te mal - i - e. Na - e ko ha - ki - li - a.)

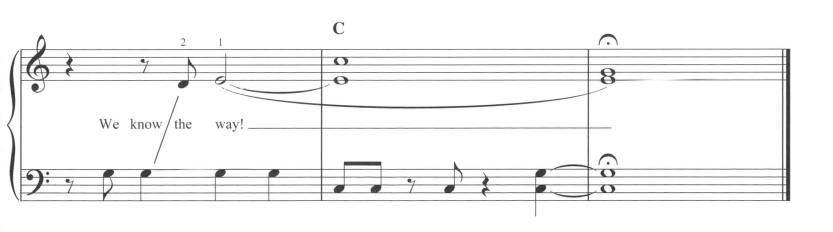

We know the way! ___

YOU'RE WELCOME

from MOANA

Music and Lyrics by
LIN-MANUEL MIRANDA

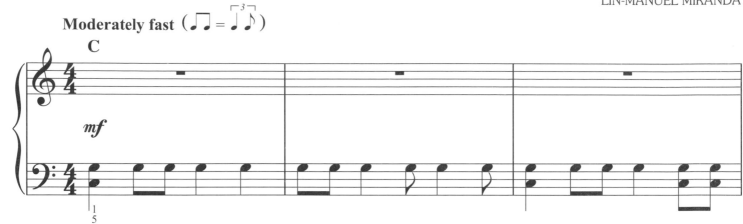

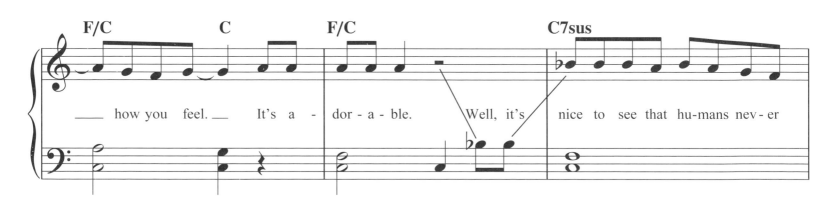

change. O - pen your eyes. Let's __ be - gin. __ Yes, it's real - ly

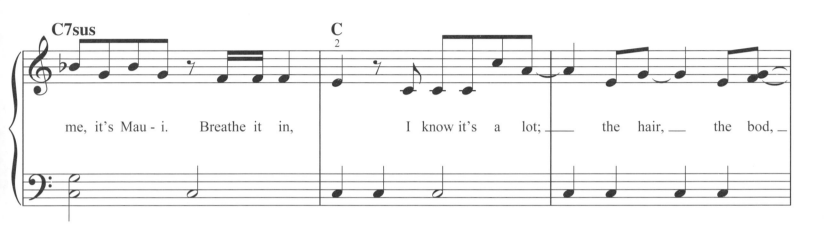

me, it's Mau - i. Breathe it in, I know it's a lot; __ the hair, __ the bod, __

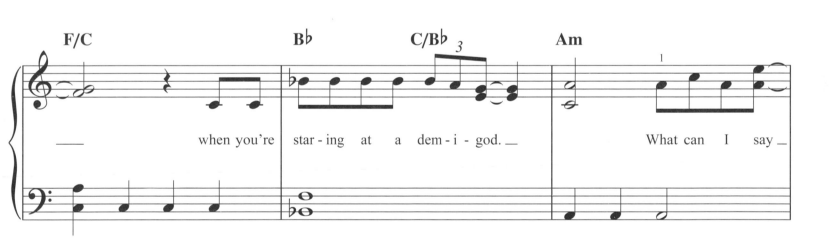

when you're star - ing at a dem - i - god. __ What can I say __

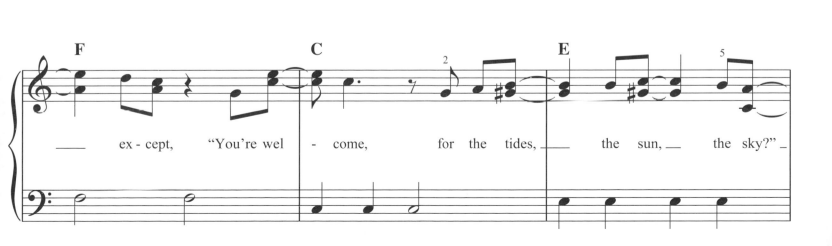

ex - cept, "You're wel - come, for the tides, __ the sun, __ the sky?" __

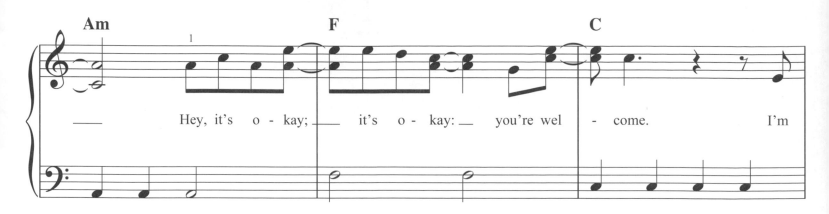

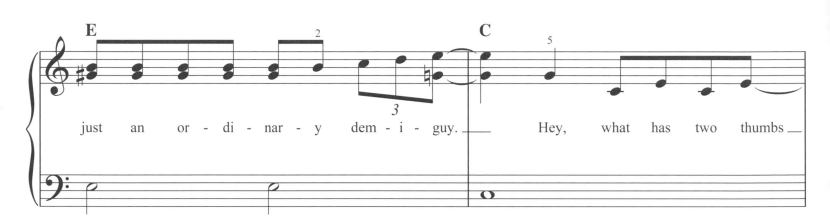

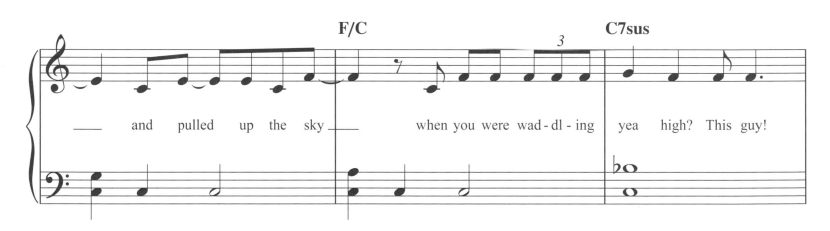

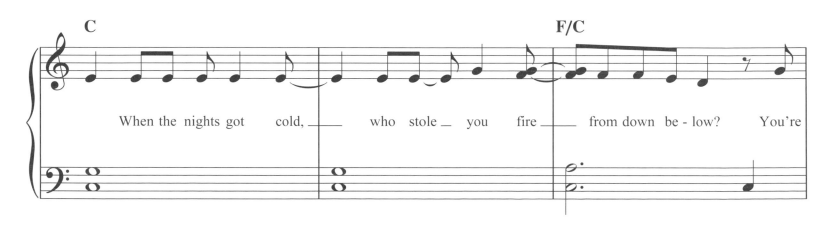

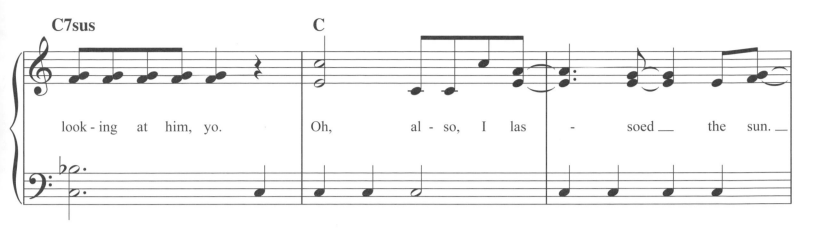

C7sus ... **C**

look - ing at him, yo. Oh, al - so, I las - soed the sun.

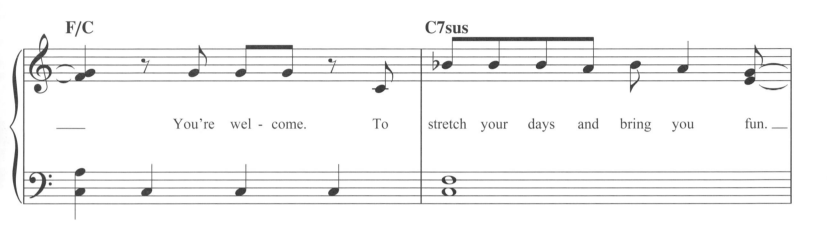

F/C ... **C7sus**

You're wel - come. To stretch your days and bring you fun.

C ... **B♭/C** **F/C**

Al - so, I har - nessed the breeze. You're wel - come. To

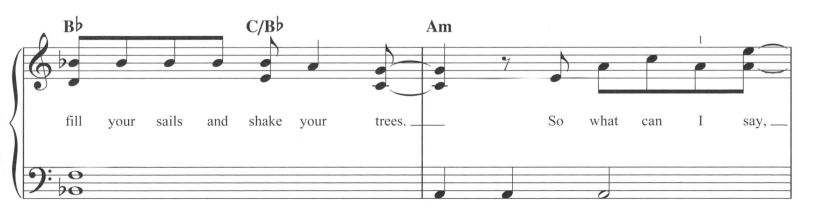

B♭ **C/B♭** **Am**

fill your sails and shake your trees. So what can I say,

ex - cept, __ "You're wel - come,   for the is - lands I pulled __ from the sea?" __

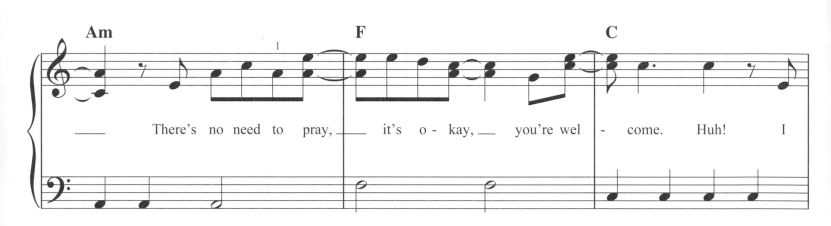

There's no need to pray, __ it's o - kay, __ you're wel - come. Huh!   I

guess it's just my way of be-ing me! __   You're wel - come!   You're wel -

- come!   *Well, come to think of it:*   *Rap: (See additional lyrics)*

Well, an - y - way, ___ let me say, ___ "You're wel -

- come, for the won - der - ful world ___ you know." ___ Hey, it's o - kay, ___

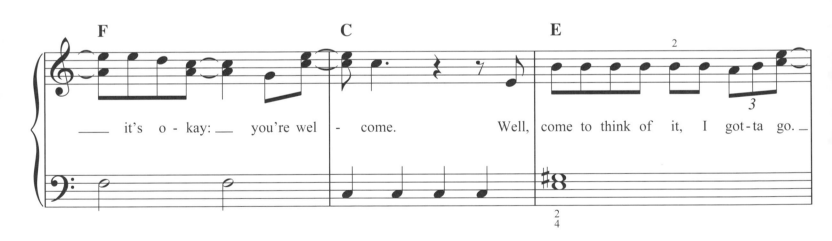

___ it's o - kay: ___ you're wel - come. Well, come to think of it, I got - ta go. ___

___ Hey, it's your day ___ to say, ___ "You're wel - come," 'cause

I'm gon-na need __ that boat. __ I'm sail-ing a-way, __ a-way. __ You're wel -

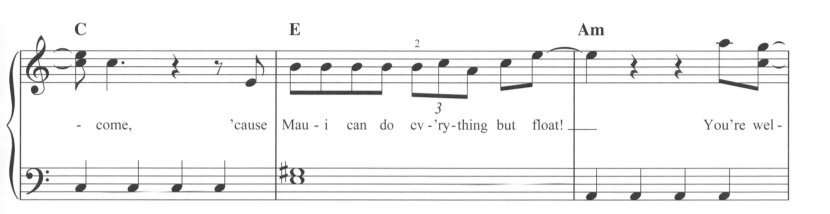

- come, 'cause Mau- i can do ev-'ry-thing but float! __ You're wel-

- come! You're wel - come! And thank you.

8vb

Additional Lyrics

Rap: Kid, honestly, I could go on and on.
I could explain ev'ry nat'ral phenomenon.
The tide? The grass? The ground?
Oh, that was Maui, just messing around.

I killed an eel, I buried its guts,
Sprouted a tree: now you got coconuts!
What's the lesson? What is the takeaway?
Don't mess with Maui when he's on a breakaway.

And the tapestry here in my skin
Is a map of the vict'ries I win!
Look where I've been! I make ev'rything happen!
Look at that mean mini Maui, just tickety
Tappin'! Heh, heh, heh,
Heh, heh, heh, hey!

I SEE THE LIGHT

from TANGLED

Music by ALAN MENKEN
Lyrics by GLENN SLATER

All those days,
Now I'm here,

watch-ing from the win-dows.
blink-ing in the star-light.

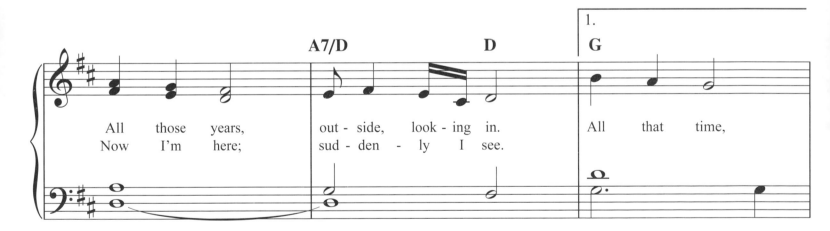

All those years,
Now I'm here;

out-side, look-ing in.
sud-den-ly I see.

All that time,

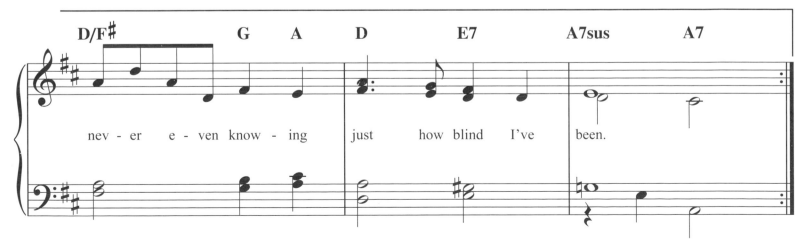

nev-er e-ven know-ing just how blind I've been.

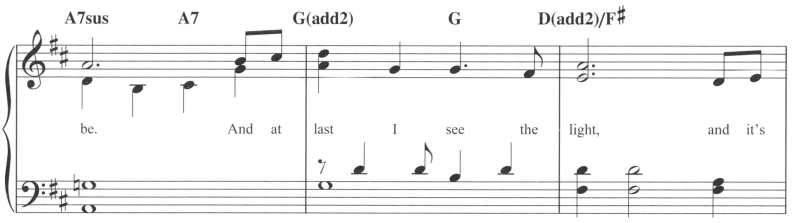

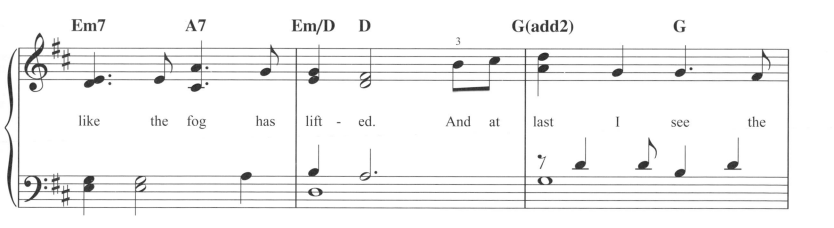

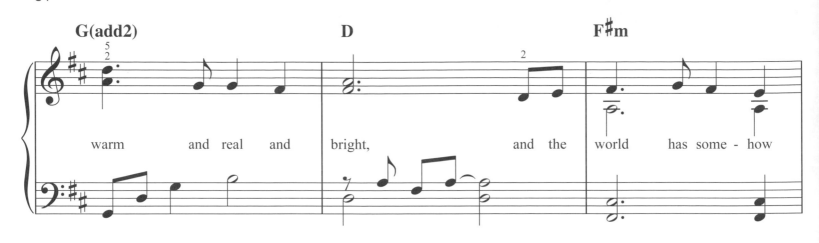

warm and real and bright, and the world has some - how

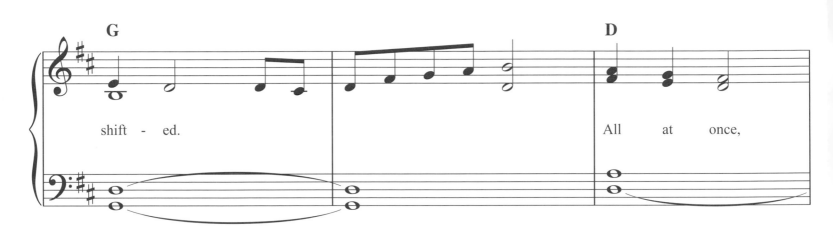

shift - ed. All at once,

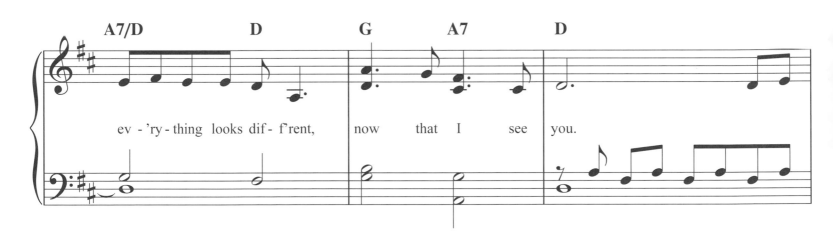

ev - 'ry - thing looks dif - f'rent, now that I see you.

All those days, chas - ing down a day - dream.

All those years liv-ing in a blur. All that time,

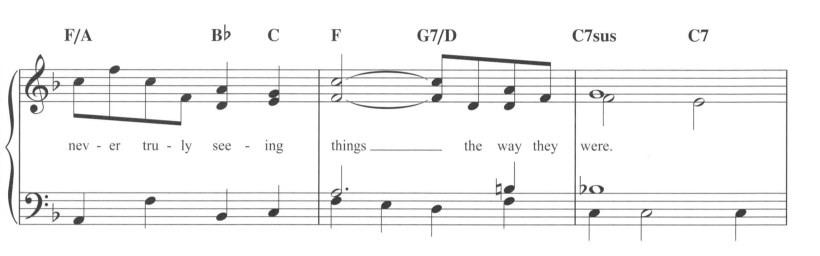

nev-er tru-ly see-ing things _____ the way they were.

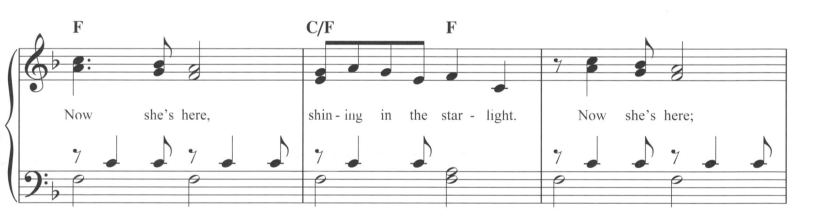

Now she's here, shin-ing in the star - light. Now she's here;

sud-den-ly I know: if she's here, it's crys - tal clear I'm

86

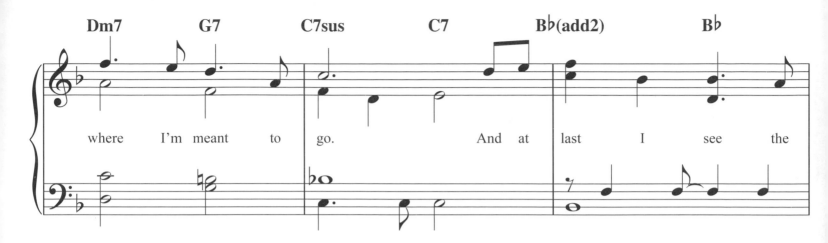

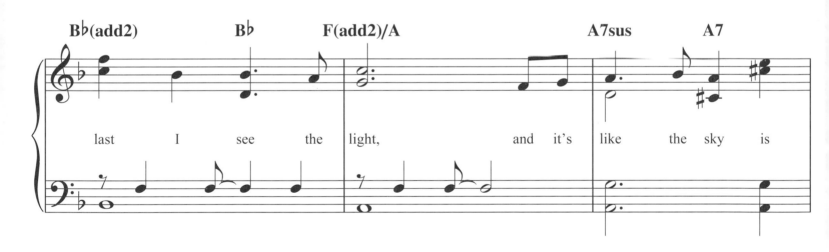

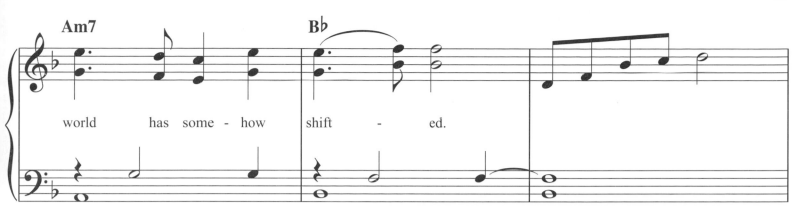

world has some-how shift - ed.

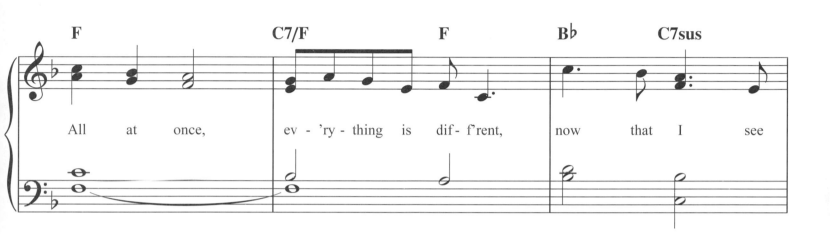

All at once, ev - 'ry - thing is dif - f'rent, now that I see

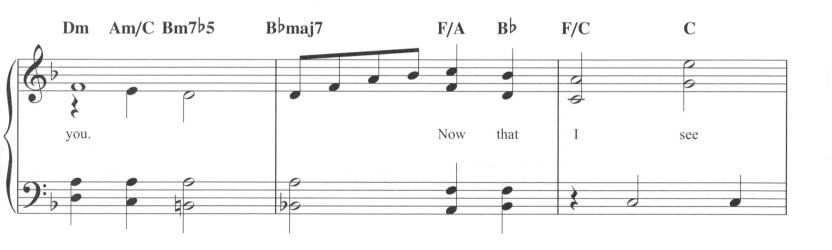

you. Now that I see

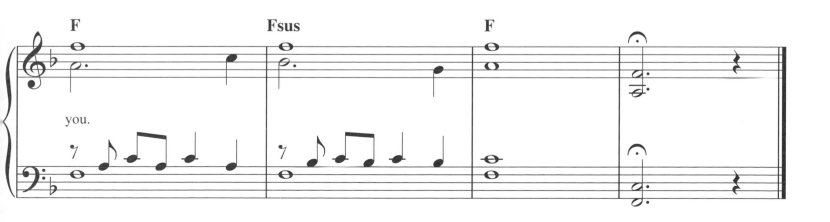

you.

I'VE GOT A DREAM
from TANGLED

Music by ALAN MENKEN
Lyrics by GLENN SLATER

HOOK HAND THUG:

I'm ma - li - cious, mean, and scar - y. My

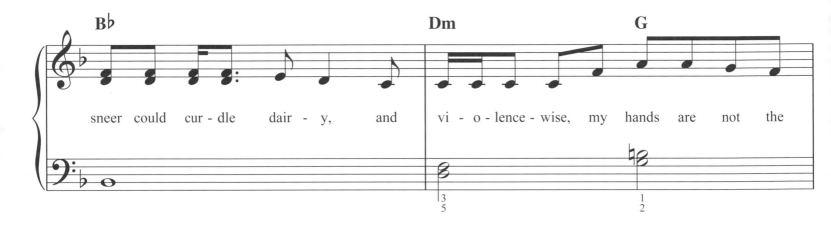

sneer could cur - dle dair - y, and vi - o - lence - wise, my hands are not the

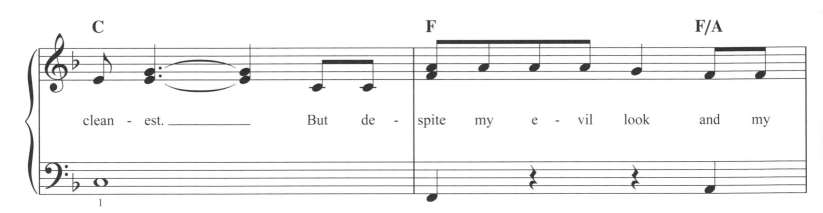

clean - est. _____ But de - spite my e - vil look and my

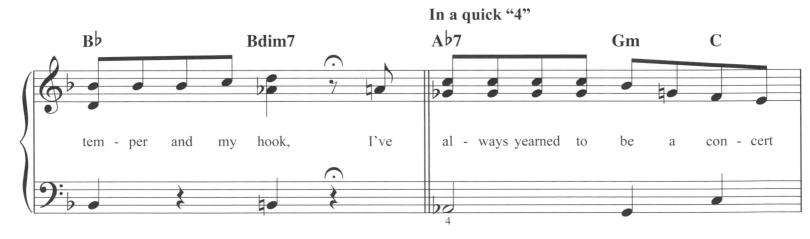

tem - per and my hook, I've al - ways yearned to be a con - cert

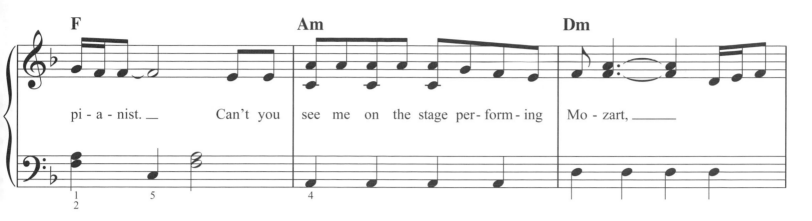

pi - a - nist. __ Can't you see me on the stage per - form - ing Mo - zart, _____

tick-l-ing the i-v'ries 'til they gleam? Yep, I'd rath-er be called dead-ly for my

kill - er show - tune med - ley. Thank you! 'Cause

way down deep in - side, I've got a dream. _____ He's got a dream, _____ he's got a

HOOK HAND THUG:

dream. See, I ain't as cruel and vi - cious as I seem. Though I

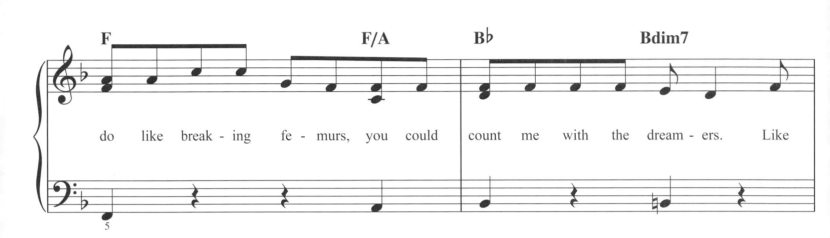

do like break - ing fe - murs, you could count me with the dream - ers. Like

THUG CHORUS:

ev - 'ry - bod - y else, I've got a dream.
Na na na na na na na na na

BIG NOSE THUG:

na na na na na. I've got scars and lumps and bruis - es, ___ plus

some - thing here that ooz - es, and let's not e - ven men - tion my com - plex - ion. _____ But de -

spite my ex - tra toes and my goi - ter and my nose, I real - ly want to make a love con -

nec - tion. _____ Can't you see me with a spe - cial lit - tle la - dy, _____

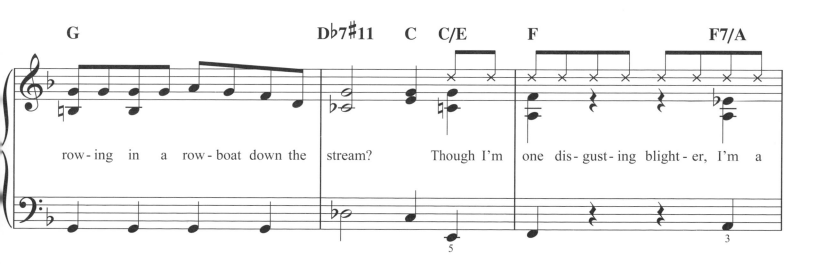

row - ing in a row - boat down the stream? Though I'm one dis - gust - ing blight - er, I'm a

lov - er, not a fight - er, 'cause way down deep in - side, I've got a dream. I've got a

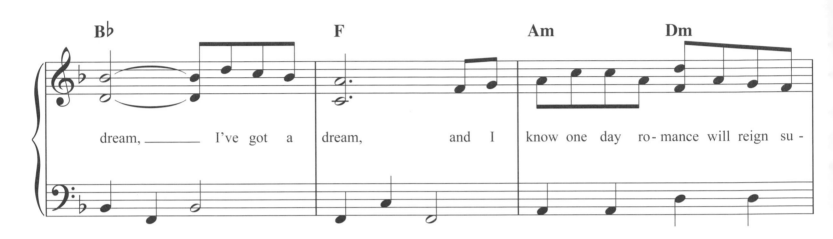

dream, _____ I've got a dream, and I know one day ro - mance will reign su -

preme! Though my face leaves peo - ple scream - ing, there's a child be - hind it dream - ing. Like

THUG CHORUS:

ev - 'ry - bod - y else, I've got a dream. Tor would like to quit and be a

flo-rist. _____ Gun-ther does in-te-ri-or de-sign.

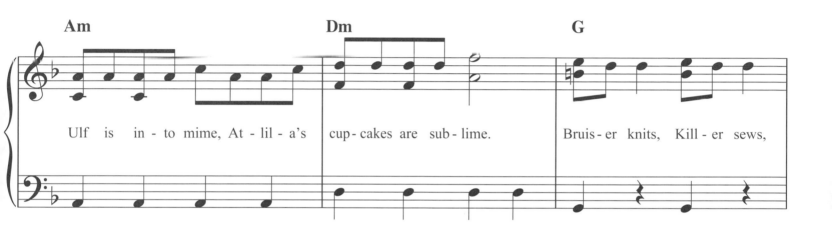

Ulf is in-to mime, At-lil-a's cup-cakes are sub-lime. Bruis-er knits, Kill-er sews,

HOOK HAND THUG:

Fang does lit-tle pup-pet shows, and Vla-di-mir col-lects cer-am-ic u - ni-corns.

rit.

FLYNN:

I have dreams like you, no, real-ly! Just much less touch-y feel-y. They

a tempo

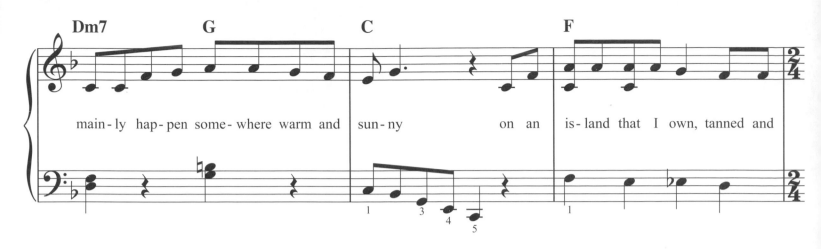

main-ly hap-pen some-where warm and sun-ny on an is-land that I own, tanned and

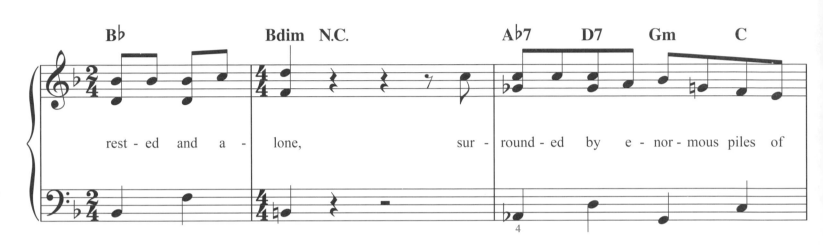

rest-ed and a - lone, sur-round-ed by e - nor-mous piles of

RAPUNZEL:

mon-ey. _____ I've got a dream, _____ I've got a dream. I just

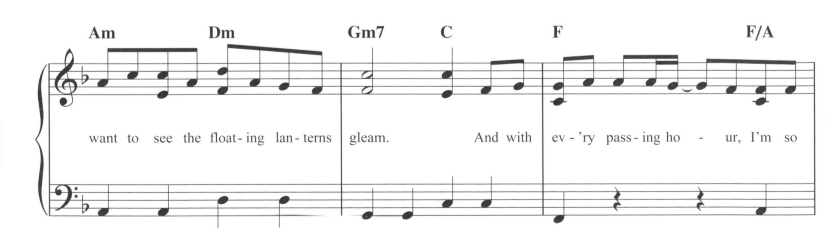

want to see the float-ing lan-terns gleam. And with ev-'ry pass-ing ho - ur, I'm so

THUG CHORUS:

glad I left my tow - er. Like all you love - ly folks, I've got a dream. _____ She's got a

dream, _____ we've got a dream. So our dif - f'renc - es ain't real - ly that ex -

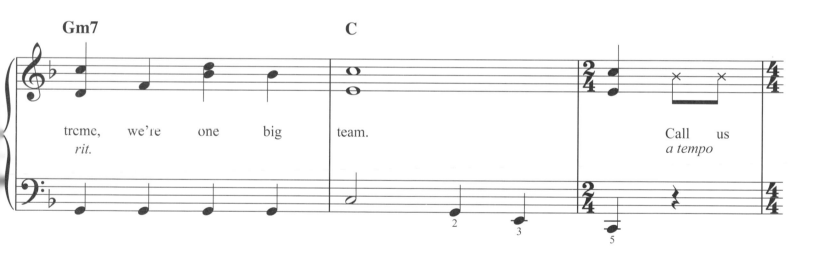

treme, we're one big team. Call us

rit. *a tempo*

bru - tal, sick, sa - dis - tic, and gro - tes - quely op - ti - mis - tic. 'Cause

way down deep in - side, we've got a dream, I've got a dream, I've got a

dream, I've got a dream, I've got a dream, I've got a dream, I've got a

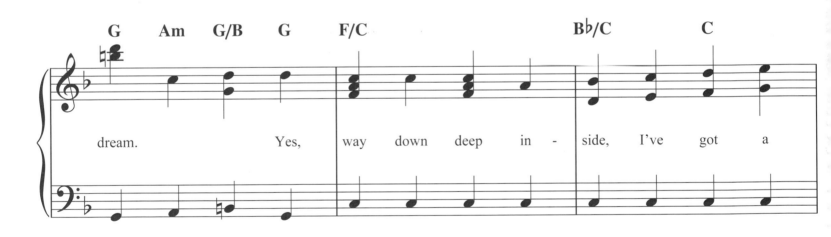

dream. Yes, way down deep in - side, I've got a

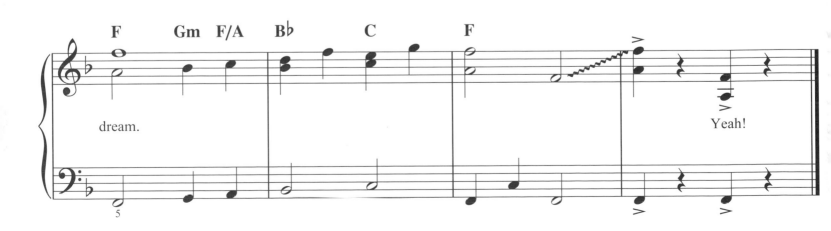

dream. Yeah!